Amazing
Modern-Day
Miracles

52 True Stories to
Strengthen Your Faith

Amazing
Modern-Day
Miracles

52 True Stories to
Strengthen Your Faith

S U Z A N N E   F R E Y

Guideposts

Danbury, Connecticut

AMAZING MODERN-DAY MIRACLES
Copyright © 2014 Suzanne Frey

Acknowledgments
Every attempt has been made to credit the sources of copyrighted material used in this book. If any such acknowledgment has been inadvertently omitted or miscredited, receipt of such information would be appreciated.

Unless otherwise indicated, Scripture quotations are taken from the Holy Bible, New International-al Version®, NIV®. Copyright © 1973, 1978, 1984, 2011 by Biblica, Inc.® Used by permission. All rights reserved worldwide.

Verses marked NLT are taken from the *Holy Bible*, New Living Translation, copyright © 1996, 2004, 2007, 2013 by Tyndale House Foundation. Used by permission of Tyndale House Publishers, Inc., Carol Stream, Illinois 60188. All rights reserved.

Verses marked NASB are taken from the New American Standard Bible®, © 1960, 1962, 1963, 1968, 1971, 1972, 1973, 1975, 1977, 1995 by The Lockman Foundation. Used by permission. (www.Lockman.org)

Verses marked NKJV are taken from the New King James Version®. Copyright © 1982 by Thomas Nelson, Inc. Used by permission. All rights reserved.

Verses marked HCSB are taken from the HCSB®, Copyright © 1999, 2000, 2002, 2003, 2009 by Holman Bible Publishers. Used by permission. HCSB® is a federally registered trademark of Holman Bible Publishers.

Verses marked ESV are from The ESV® Bible (The Holy Bible, English Standard Version®), copyright © 2001 by Crossway, a publishing ministry of Good News Publishers. Used by permission. All rights reserved.

Verses marked MSG are taken from THE MESSAGE. Copyright © by Eugene H. Peterson 1993, 1994, 1995, 1996, 2000, 2001, 2002. Used by permission of Tyndale House Publishers, Inc.

Cover by Serena Fox, Serena Fox Design Company/Bean, Inc.
Cover photo: iStockphoto.com

The incidents described in this book are true. Where individuals may be identifiable, they have granted the author and the publisher the right to use their names, stories, and/or facts of their lives in all manners, including composite or altered representations. In all other cases, names, circumstances, descriptions, and details have been changed to render individuals unidentifiable.

This Guideposts edition is published by special arrangement with Harvest House Publishers.

Printed in the United States of America
10 9 8 7 6 5 4 3 2 1

To my incredible family:

Ron, Stephen, Lauren, and Katie

ACKNOWLEDGMENTS

My deepest gratitude to…

my family—Ron, Stephen, Lauren, and Katie—for believing in me and in this project. Your ideas, encouragement, and assistance have been invaluable. Lauren, as managing editor, your giftedness in writing and countless hours of editing shine through each story.

my Moms in Prayer friends, whom I've had the privilege of praying with for the past several years. Together, we've experienced the joy of pouring our hearts out to God, and we have seen Him, in incredible and unforgettable ways, answer our prayers.

my Toastmasters friends in the Noon Talkers and Speak Life clubs. You have taught me the power of telling a story well and helped me learn how to tell mine with skill and confidence.

my extended family and friends—thank you for your ongoing love, support, and prayers.

the contributors who have shared your stories with courage, transparency, and integrity—this book couldn't have happened without you and your faith.

my editorial assistance team—Carey Chmarny, Ron Frey, David Sanford—for the gift of your time and counsel.

Jesus, knowing You and experiencing Your love is the greatest joy in my life.

CONTENTS

God's Amazing Love for Us

God's Amazing Love for Us

When my three children were very young, our family traveled to Washington, DC, to visit its famous monuments and memorials. In preparation for our trip, we checked out picture- and historical-fact books and immersed ourselves in the history of each memorial and its significance to our nation. We felt this was one way we could truly appreciate what our eyes would be beholding. We recognized that these monuments tell important stories.

The idea of building monuments to remember past events is nothing new. In the Old Testament of the Bible, God told His people to build memorials around significant events and miraculous deliverances He had orchestrated. These memorials not only served as significant reminders to the nation of Israel, but they were also meant to bear witness to the surrounding tribes and countries, in essence stating, "This is who our God is." Many references to the monuments include, "And that stone is still there today." Psalm 145:4-6 says:

> Generation after generation stands in awe of your work; each one tells stories of your mighty acts. Your beauty and splendor have everyone talking...Your marvelous doings are headline news; I could write a book full of the details of your greatness. (MSG)

These verses—and the desire to share how amazing God is—became the basis for *Amazing Modern-Day Miracles*. It is my hope that as you read these stories, you'll walk with the contributors through their unique, challenging, and poignant circumstances as they talked with God and trusted Him for the outcome.

My heart for this book is to echo the placing of monuments by God's people. I value these testimonies of God so much that I wanted to write them down so we could pause to reflect and remember Who loves us and note the marvelous ways He answers our prayers.

I pray that you'll be encouraged by the stories of each of these contributors and let their journeys lead you to better know and love the Miracle Maker.

May God bless you in your own journey.

Suzanne Frey

In the final stages of this book project, after the fifty-two stories were set and ready for publishing, the unexpected hit our family. What quickly unfolded was one of the most challenging and faith-stretching seasons of my life. After seeing how God provided for countless others, we were about to see Him work in our lives. Here is the story.

RARE, COMPLICATED, AND DEADLY

"Hey, I've had a health issue and need to explain it to you. Can we talk?" announced the text message from our twenty-five-year-old son. Ron, my husband, immediately phoned Stephen, whose voice was barely audible: "I've got a sore throat and they say I need surgery."

Stephen handed the phone to the emergency-room doctor who explained the diagnosis: "He's got necrotizing fasciitis, and we're going to have to operate. We'll put a tracheotomy in his throat so he can breathe, and get him into the first operating room available."

Necrotizing what? I quickly looked it up online at WebMD and read that it's an aggressive, "flesh-eating" disease that destroys soft tissue. Then I saw…"Can lead to amputation and death." My heart stopped. *He's got this in his throat?*

How can this be? The weekend before, we were together at a wedding, and Stephen was healthy, energetic, and dancing the night away with his sisters. But now, while out of town, he came down with a terrible sore throat. Unable to shake it, Stephen checked himself into the emergency room at the nearest hospital.

I was terrified. Stephen was in a very precarious position. A few hours' delay, and he may die. My husband and I pleaded with God to save his life, and we immediately sent text messages to family and close friends informing them of Stephen's condition, asking them to join us in praying for his survival.

The next morning we were on the first plane flight out to see him. As we walked into the intensive care unit, Stephen greeted us with his good-natured smile. He was hooked up to a spaghetti maze of tubes coming out or going into just about every body part. A five-inch horizontal incision across his neck combined with a tracheotomy tube in his swollen throat, displayed the result of his infection and emergency surgery the night before.

We learned the bacteria infection was streptococcus anginosus. We all carry normal bacteria in our mouths, but every once in awhile it can get infected. This is what happened. The infection grew rapidly and made abscesses of pus and bacteria like a ball. Antibiotics alone can't fix it because the blood vessels don't penetrate the pocket of pus, so it needs surgery to be drained. There is nothing Stephen did to contract this disease, nor was it contagious. But the severity of his condition was very rare and complicated.

Two days later he had another neck surgery. A CT scan showed the infection had spread to his chest, and the only way to get rid of it was for the doctor to open up his chest and clean it out. The following day, they washed the infection out of his heart sac, lungs, and sternum.

After four surgeries in seven days, we expected Stephen to improve. Instead, his skin was ashen, and he looked like he was dying. The doctor told us he was in extreme danger, and cases like his have a 50-percent chance of survival. With this news, I crumpled over Ron in tears. We called out to God to save Stephen's life.

We created an Internet health journal and posted regular updates and prayer requests asking family and close friends to pray for Stephen's survival and a turnaround in his infection. Soon there were more than 160 people praying for him every day. The next day was Sunday, and five churches prayed for Stephen. One church even stopped their service for thirty minutes to pray for him! Many people around the city and our country joined us in prayer that day too. We later learned that this was the very day that his necrotizing fasciitis and streptococcus anginosus no longer showed up in the lab work. A major answer to prayer!

Each day there were positive signs, but by the end of the second week, Stephen was still in very serious condition. Seeing our six-foot-five, strong, independent, and determined son confined to a bed with a maze of tubes coming out of him became the new normal. The days ran together as I stood and sat by his hospital bed twelve, thirteen, sometimes even fourteen hours each day.

While gazing at his precious face and stroking his arm, I realized it had been years since I had spent this many hours with my son. I wished it were under different circumstances. Still, as his mom, I cherished being near him, watching him sleep, praying for him, and holding his hand. I was thankful for the comfort it seemed to bring him, and grateful my voice and my touch could calm him.

I typed copious notes on my laptop as his medical teams continually passed through his room, reporting his status and vitals and their concerns and treatments.

Then I was told a second life-threatening bacterial infection, klebsiella pneumoniae, had invaded his lungs and was growing near his heart, causing his condition to worsen. He had many moments of coughing and uneasy breathing while hooked up to a ventilator. His blood pressure, temperature, and white blood count all were abnormal.

I prayed several short prayers over him.

Lord, heal Stephen. Remove every infected cell in his body. Revive him in every way. Destroy and eliminate all the infections. Keep them from spreading. Let the antibiotics do their job. Give the surgeons supernatural wisdom and ability to wash, clean out, and remove everything contaminating his body. Restore his body to wholeness.

It brought me comfort knowing that I was not the only one praying these prayers. Our family and friends joined us in praying intently for his discharge from the ICU, and eventually the hospital. They continued to reach out, praying, sending texts, e-mails, and posting comments on our health journal. I read these comments over and over, and they sustained me. God embraced me through our family and friends; I was carried by love.

The thoracic surgeon said it was not safe for a chest to be opened for more than a week. But after several clean-out surgeries that week, she decided it would be best not to sew up his chest because of all the infection remaining. As Stephen went into surgery that night, we sent out a call to pray for the infection to be completely gone.

As the red bar on the medical board signaled that his surgery was in the closure stage, I waited and waited for the doctor to come out of the operating room. Normally it doesn't take so long. I wondered—could it be possible that she was actually sewing him up? Several minutes later, the doctor came out and said, "I sewed up his chest after all! I felt it was the right thing to do and the right time. There was less infection than I originally thought." I told her that's what we had been praying for. She grinned and said, "Well that's what you got."

The next day, Stephen felt heavy pain in his chest from the surgery closure. He said if felt like a cage was pushing in on it. Two of Ron's friends (who had never met Stephen) drove twelve hours to the hospital, sensing God was leading them to pray for Stephen. When they arrived, Stephen explained the pain in his chest, so they laid their hands on him and prayed for him and for that pain. The next morning I asked Stephen, "Do you have any pain in your chest?" He shook his head no. I asked him the same question in the evening, and his answer was the same—no pain! Two days later, Ron asked the physician to take him completely off of pain medication. The chest pain never appeared again. It was gone the day after Ron's friends had prayed.

Three days later, a CT scan showed Stephen still had some infection directly above his heart and behind his sternum, the very place where he had been sewn up the week before. We asked people to pray that there would be no infection. That evening, as he went into his eighth surgery, we prayed Psalm 51:10 over his body: "Create in me a clean heart, O God" (NLT). That evening the doctor came out of the operating room and said there was no infection—no pus! Nothing. It was gone.

Stephen spent two more weeks in the hospital after this surgery for observation and infection monitoring. Overall he had eight surgeries in twenty-five days; he had spent twenty-one days in the intensive care unit and seventeen days in the hospital for a total of five weeks.

One of the incredible ways God took care of me while Stephen was in the hospital was through a family who lived close to the hospital. I had never met them before. They graciously opened their home for me to stay with them. They even let me borrow their car to drive to and from the hospital each day. Then when Stephen was released from the hospital, this family let him stay with them as well for rehabilitation and so he could be near his doctors.

It is said that normally, rehabilitation takes three days for every one day spent in the hospital. That would add up to 114 days in rehab, but Stephen's recovery was only 31 days!

God answered many prayers, not just for Stephen's health but also for all of our financial needs. Stephen's student health insurance covered the majority of medical bills. The portion that was not covered was paid through generous gifts from family and friends and a financial-aid grant from the hospital.

And Stephen, having just graduated from college, was in the middle of projects that were leading to income. While he was in the hospital, one of his colleagues, who had no idea Stephen was in the hospital, asked him to join a project team that offered paying work. Stephen started working on neuroscience research part-time while he was still in recovery!

We prayed Stephen out of the ICU, then out of the hospital, then out of recovery. As people prayed, his circumstances changed. Today Stephen is a walking miracle, back to his adventurous, inquisitive, and productive life!

Never before had we experienced so profoundly the power of prayer. Our network of prayer warriors carried our burden with us. They rejoiced with us. They walked with us through some of our darkest days; and because of them, we have never felt alone. We are so grateful for the power of prayer and for the community of Christ.

Shout joyful praises to God, all the earth!
Sing about the glory of his name!
Tell the world how glorious he is.
Say to God, 'How awesome are your deeds!'
Come and see what our God has done,
what awesome miracles he performs for his people!
Psalm 66:1-3, 5 NLT

1

The Jungle Horse

JERRY LONG

One day my ten-year-old daughter, Lori, came to me and said, "Daddy, when I grow up, I want to raise horses. Can I have a horse?" At the time, my family and I were living in Limoncocha, the jungle center of operations for Wycliffe Bible Translators in Ecuador.

A horse? I thought. Living in the Amazon, Lori already had every animal imaginable. One day I counted seventeen critters in, around, under, and swinging from the rafters of our house. A calf from a local farm project was staked in our backyard, and there was an alligator in my shower stall.

"Honey," I said, "first of all, we can't afford a horse. Even if we could, the only way into our community is by boat or airplane. So the only way a horse could get here is either by flying or swimming. Besides, I don't know if horses can adapt to the jungle. They don't strike me as jungle animals."

Lori cried. She *really* wanted a horse.

So I said, "Honey, if you want a horse that badly, you need to talk to God about it. He's the only one I know who can arrange it."

So Lori took my advice and talked to God.

A few weeks later, I was handed a teletype message from Quito, the capital city of Ecuador. It was addressed to our neighbor, Otto Rodrigues, who had a hacienda—a large estate—about thirty miles upriver. The letter was from his attorney telling him he needed to get into the city as soon as possible for some business transactions. It looked urgent enough that I asked one of our pilots to fly me over to Otto's place so I could do a message drop.

As we flew over Otto's property, I noticed a horse grazing among his cattle. I thought, *How about that! There's a horse that survives in the jungle. I'll have to tell Lori.*

About a week later, one of our Indian workers came to my door.

"Señor Long," he said, "you won't believe what is coming down the river. There is a raft made of two dugout canoes with a platform on them—a platform with a *horse* tied on it."

A little later that day, a man came to my door leading the horse. He said: "Don Otto so appreciates his friends here at the mission that he sent this horse, thinking the kids would enjoy having him."

For the rest of our time at Limoncocha, Lori spent nearly all her days with that horse. This was God's gift to her!

Today Lori boards, breeds, and trains Arabian horses on her property in Oregon. Better yet, she still believes in prayer.

> *Ask and it will be given to you; seek and you will find; knock and the door will be opened to you. (Matthew 7:7)*

Jerry Long served forty-three years with Wycliffe Bible Translators as a writer, administrator, and international training consultant. In his retirement he founded Kingdom Come Training, which uses live, interactive videoconferencing to train and coach missionaries to achieve their full funding quickly.

2

The Occult Store

PRISCILLA SHIRER

Jaye Martin is a mother who lives in Houston, Texas. When I met her, I was captivated as she shared the story about a store that opened near her child's elementary school. The shop was known for selling merchandise connected to the occult. In addition, Jaye and others in the community were fairly certain that illegal drugs were being sold there.

At the time, Jaye was a part of a moms' group that prayed for the protection of their children. And now these children were spending much of their day close to that store. When the moms discovered that some of the children were wandering over to it after school and becoming interested in its wares, Jaye went to see the store owner to express her concern.

The store owner assured her there was no harm in what he was offering and, besides, he was breaking no laws. Despite her request that he find a location better suited to his products and the community, he refused to consider leaving.

Undeterred, Jaye called the leasing agent and asked him to reconsider the lease because of the close proximity to the elementary school. He explained that he didn't see a reason not to allow the store owner to rent the space. Jaye, fed up with the obvious spiritual opposition, replied matter-of-factly, "Well, then, we will just have to pray them out."

At the next prayer meeting, she introduced the concept of not just praying for their children's safety, but praying the occult store out of the neighborhood. The other mothers were stunned at the thought of using prayer as a direct weapon. It was a new concept for many of them. But together, in faith, they prayed fervently that heaven would intervene on their behalf.

Two months later, the occult store was gone.

Truly I tell you that if two of you on earth agree about anything they ask for, it will be done for them by my Father in heaven. (Matthew 18:19)

Copied by permission from Priscilla Shirer, Beth Moore, and Kay Arthur, *Anointed Transformed Redeemed: A Study of David* (Nashville: LifeWay Christian Resources, 2008), p. 48. Edited and used with permission.

Priscilla Shirer, a speaker and author, has spent more than a decade addressing corporations, organizations, and Christian audiences across the United States and around the world.

3

Scandalous Love

JAY A. BARBER, JR.

It was the early winter of 1983. I was headed south from Portland, Oregon, to California on business in our recently acquired used Chevy custom van—you know, the kind with the captain chairs, the swing-up table, and, in the back, a bench seat that collapsed into a bed. I was nearing Cottage Grove, Oregon, when all of a sudden the alternator warning light began burning brightly. I'd just noticed billboards along the highway advertising Uncle Bud's Chevrolet dealership. I still had a long trip ahead of me, so I decided to go there to have the alternator checked out.

As I turned over the keys to the manager, he invited me to sit down in the waiting room. It was going to be awhile because others were in line before me. I didn't think about it at the time, but I'd left my briefcase in the car. I could have been doing some work while I waited, but instead I picked up a magazine that had been left on the table for the customers to read. Little did I know how important reading that magazine would be.

One week later, on a dark and cold December night, I was heading north to Portland, anxious to get home to my wife and family. Ice and snow lined the roadside and snow flurried about.

I drove through Weed, California, and was just beyond the

final exit to the town when I saw two figures standing on the road-side. One of them had a thumb out as I passed by. I could tell they were wrapped in a blanket that was shielding them from the ice and snow.

Now, I had a policy that I would never pick up hitchhikers. But to my own amazement, I found myself slamming on the brakes and pulling to the side of the freeway. In my rearview mirror, I saw the two figures I assumed were a man and a woman running toward me through the snow. I was at least a hundred yards down the freeway, so I backed up to meet them. When they got close, I stopped and turned on the overhead light in the van. I then stepped outside into the freezing wind, walked around the car, and slid the old van door open.

As they approached, I got the surprise of my life. It wasn't a man and a woman, but two men wrapped up in the blanket. One of them thrust a small bundle from their arms into mine. I looked down at the bundle in the overhead light and saw a small child—a little girl. As I looked into her angelic face, terror struck my heart. Her face was blue. Without thinking, I cried, "This child is dead! This child is dead!"

One of the two men began to cry and scream hysterically. The other man climbed into my van. I shouted orders to the man who was crying. "Get her cold and wet clothing off! You!" I pointed to the other man. "You take off your coat, your shirt—get down to your bare skin. Put her body next to yours! There's a bed in the back where you can lie down. I'll head for the hospital!" I didn't realize it at the time, but we were on a lone stretch of highway and the next exit where we could get help was many miles away. As I drove, it looked hopeless.

"O God," I prayed, "save that precious little girl." As I sped down the freeway, praying every mile of the way, I began to hear the most beautiful sound in the world—whimpering. Pretty soon, the child began to scream and cry with gusto. She was alive! She was going to be okay.

As we traveled north, I discovered that the father and his friend lived in Corvallis, Oregon. The father had only recently discovered he was indeed the father of the child. He'd also received the news that the mother of the child was going to prison. Unless he went to Texas to claim his parental rights and responsibilities, the child would be placed in long-term foster care. When he got this news, he and his buddy decided to hitchhike all the way to Texas to get the child. Then they planned to hitchhike back to Corvallis.

To this day I often think about and pray for that little girl, who would now be in her thirties. I wonder what she's done with her life. I especially think about her at Christmastime, and not just because the story of Christmas is also about a small child on a cold and blustery night. No, it's because in many ways the little girl with the blue face, in the late stages of hypothermia, represents you and me.

Like the little girl, we were without hope. We were "dead in our trespasses and sins" (Ephesians 2:1) until Jesus, the Son of God, came to save us. Through His Son, God took us into His scandalous love. He rescued us into the warmth of His arms. He knew exactly what we needed in order to be saved.

And God knew exactly what that little girl needed to live too. What was in that magazine I read in the waiting room at Uncle Bud's Chevrolet dealership? The article was all about what a person needs to know and do to treat hypothermia.

Put your hope in the LORD, for with the LORD is unfailing love and with him is full redemption. (Psalm 130:7)

Jay A. Barber, Jr. is president emeritus of Warner Pacific College, Portland, Oregon.

4

Ugly Soup in a Pickle Jar

SUSAN GUENTHER

It was only a matter of time. Scott, my neighbor and a wonderful husband and father, had stopped responding to the treatment for brain cancer. Besides praying for Scott and his family every time they came to mind, I decided the most practical thing I could do to show them love would be to anonymously deliver meals in disposable containers to their front doorstep. That way they wouldn't have to invite me in to visit or worry about returning my dishes.

Over the next several months, I covered their doorstep with homemade pies, cookies, soups, breads, and freezer jams—anything I thought might taste good to them. However, as we heard reports of the cancer progressing, it became more and more challenging to figure out what foods might be appealing to Scott as his condition was declining.

One afternoon, as I was wracking my brains for something Scott might like, I suddenly thought of split-pea soup.

I got busy assembling the ingredients, but abruptly paused when I realized that I only had yellow split peas. *Yellow split peas taste pretty much the same as green split peas,* I thought. So I continued whipping up the soup. Yet when it was finished, it looked like a mess. It tasted good, but it was *really* ugly. I decided to put the ugly looking soup into a clean, glass pickle jar I had been planning to recycle. When I poured the soup into the pickle jar, it looked even more unattractive. Hoping to spruce up the looks of it a bit, I tied raffia ribbon around the lid and tucked in a small wild rose. But it was not an improvement.

I looked at the clock. It was after six in the evening. *Too late for a thoughtful dinner drop-off*, I thought to myself, feeling like I had wasted time making ugly soup that I didn't even have the nerve to give away due to the lateness of the hour and its homely appearance. "Thanks for the great inspiration," I mumbled to God in a sarcastic tone. I shoved the soup into the fridge, feeling like a lousy neighbor and bratty child of God.

The next day, however, I strongly felt God telling me to give the ugly soup to Scott. So I walked over to their house and dropped it off at the front door with some bread and jam, hoping to make a mad dash and not be seen. But as God would have it, a family friend of theirs was leaving just as I was dropping off my gift. Scott's wife saw me through the open door and invited me to bring the food into the kitchen.

Scott's wife seemed overwhelmed, sad, angry, and frustrated—everything I would imagine feeling if my husband were dying of cancer. As I set the items on her counter, she eyed the ugly soup in the pickle jar with raised eyebrows as if to say, *What on earth is that?* I was immediately embarrassed.

"This is yellow split-pea soup," I said. I rambled on, apologizing for how ugly it looked in the pickle jar. But I didn't get far into my apology because as soon as I said, "yellow split-pea soup," Scott's wife broke down in tears. She asked, "How did you know?"

How did I know what? I wondered. She had to gather herself and gulp back sobs before she could tell me the story.

Earlier that morning, Scott had told her that the only thing that sounded good to him to eat was split-pea soup. She'd angrily replied that with all the friends and family coming and going to visit, chat, and pray with him to cheer him up, she simply didn't have time to make him soup. Later she felt bad for snapping at him, especially since he hardly ever asked for such specific items.

"God knew you were going to make it and bring it just when Scott wanted it," she finished.

Then I tearfully explained that I had made it the night before, but I didn't bring it because it was too late for dinner and I was too embarrassed over its appearance.

"You brought it at the perfect time—and it's beautiful," she replied.

A few weeks later, I attended Scott's memorial service. Just before the service started, Scott's wife grabbed me and proudly introduced me to the pastor and Scott's dad as "the split-pea soup lady." Both men smiled and hugged me, thanking me for being a generous and supportive neighbor.

I've since learned not to question God when He gives me a specific task to do. Even when it feels inadequate, unimportant, or mundane. God often uses the simple, humble, and ordinary things to bless others. We shouldn't deny someone a blessing because we feel our gift is unworthy. God makes all our offerings acceptable and pleasing when they are given with a right heart, whether they seem ugly—as ugly as yellow split-pea soup in a pickle jar—or not.

Each of you should give what you have decided in your heart to give, not reluctantly or under compulsion, for God loves a cheerful giver. (2 Corinthians 9:7)

Susan Guenther still enjoys making homemade soup. She and her husband have been teaching Sunday school to two- and three-year-olds for more than twenty years.

5

Soccer Balls from Heaven

Michele Perry

I am a Florida girl by birth. I think mascara belongs in a survival kit, and my idea of camping is a day spa. But one day God called me to move to a dusty border town called Yei, nestled in the far recesses of the bush of what is now South Sudan, along the borders of the Democratic Republic of the Congo and Uganda. When I moved there, I did what everyone told me was crazy: I opened a rescue home for orphaned and abandoned children in what was still active guerilla-warfare territory. Over my seven years establishing the base there, the children's rescue home grew to more than a hundred children. (It continues to help many hundreds more.)

Soon after I arrived, I heard, "*Mama, Mama, Mama, nina deru footballs.*" ("We want footballs.") I replied, "*Aye, ana arif itakum deru footballs.*" ("Yes, I know you guys want footballs.") At that point, however, I could not give them footballs (what Americans call soccer balls). It was not that I didn't want to; we just didn't have the money for them. We barely had enough money for food. I didn't have the ability to give them this desire of their hearts, but I knew Someone who did!

So we embarked on an evening ritual of sorts. For three weeks the boys came up to me every day asking for footballs. At about four in the afternoon, a small group headed by one of the older boys would come knocking on my door. "Mama, we want footballs," he'd announce.

I would explain that I couldn't give them footballs, but that I wanted them to have footballs too.

They would smile, and then I would suggest, "Let's stop and ask Papa for footballs." (Papa is my term of endearment for our Father God. He is our Papa in heaven. You might call it my personal, contemporary English version of the Hebrew word *Abba*.) "I cannot give them to you right now, but He can."

So diligently, every day, afternoon and evening, a concerted prayer effort for footballs swept the compound. I marveled as I watched God's hand in motion. There was something much bigger at play than a potential game of soccer.

Our part of Africa has no postal service or banking infrastructure. If we want to collect our mail or withdraw necessary funds, we must embark on an eight-hour trip to Uganda over unpaved, often inaccessible roads in territory plagued with regional instabilities. It was time for another trip, and I hoped the transfer of funds would be there to greet me. Our "family" had enough food for three days. It would take me one day to travel, one day to do the business needed, and one day to return. I was cutting it close.

I left a visiting friend to oversee the compound in my absence. I waved goodbye as I walked out of the gate to the bus stop in the predawn light. Soon I was bouncing on my way along bumpy roads on a bus, surrounded by goats and chickens. I was the only Westerner for miles. As the large metal monster creaked and groaned its way closer to the city where our bank was located, I prayed silently, *Jesus, please take care of my kids. Please let the money be there.* Eight hours later we rolled into the dusty border town of Arua, which is our nearest contact with the outside fiscal world. I found a room at a local guesthouse and fell into a dreamless sleep.

The next morning I made my way to the bank. My heart sank

when I realized the transfer had not arrived yet. We had such a small window of time. *Jesus, please do something!* I sent word to the compound that I was delayed, and my prayers were echoed back home as food supplies dwindled. Even if the money came the next day, it would be another two days before I reached home.

On day three, the "mamas" at home cooked the last food in the storeroom. We could only wait to see what God would do. A virtual world away from my children, I was completely helpless and could do nothing but pray.

That day the money did arrive, but I couldn't get back any sooner than the following evening. Pictures of my hungry children ran through my mind's eye. *Jesus, help them.*

When I arrived home the following day I was unsure of what I would find. Having not eaten in almost two days, would the children be crying from hunger? Would the staff be upset? Would the visitors be on the next plane out? I didn't know. I honestly didn't expect what I found! I was greeted by beaming faces and excited voices bubbling over to tell me the story of what God had done. I should have known the heart of our Papa in heaven better!

The day before, at lunchtime, they had cooked and eaten the last bit of food in the house. As dinnertime neared the children began to pray. Not long afterward a truck honked at the gate. At that time our ministry was less than two months old, and few people knew we were there. Yet into our compound pulled a pickup truck filled with USAID food and supplies—and the driver asked for us by name!

My visiting friend was skeptical at first. She informed them clearly that we had no money with which to pay for the supplies.

"No, no—you do not understand. Your compound is on our distribution list. We just need your signature. We *have* to deliver this food to you." Amid shouts of joy from our family, the USAID men began to offload huge sacks of beans and rice and sugar. Dinner was served! And it only got better.

One of the men stood on the back of the truck and quieted the cheering crowd. "We heard you had kids here and thought you might have a use for these...." He pulled out a huge sack of— you guessed it!—soccer balls. Our kids began to jump, dance, clap, and shriek with delight.

"Wait, wait! If you like these," he said as he held up the soccer balls, "then we thought you might also like these." With that, he held up a second sack overflowing with soccer jerseys. The squeals of glee might have been heard clear up to Juba.

I arrived home to find my children eating their favorite meal of beans and rice. Then they played a game of soccer in the mud wearing their new soccer jerseys.

Indeed, there was something much bigger at play! Jesus was strengthening my faith. He was proving to me that He really would take care of our little family. He was showing us all that He is concerned with not just our basic needs but our deepest hearts' desires as well. That still undoes me when I think of it. Our children have never forgotten how Papa fed them and brought them soccer balls from heaven. Neither have I. In His kingdom, there is truly more than enough.

"So do not worry, saying, 'What shall we eat?' or 'What shall we drink?' or 'What shall we wear?'...Your heavenly Father knows that you need them. But seek first his kingdom and his righteousness, and all these things will be given to you." (Matthew 6:31-33)

Excerpted from Michele Perry, *Love Has a Face* (New York: Chosen Books/ Baker Publishing Group, 2009), pp. 122-25. Edited and used by permission.

Born without her left hip, leg, and a kidney, **Michele Perry** is no stranger to impossibilities. She established and led an international ministry base for Iris Global, including a children's rescue home, school, and network of churches, as she served in South Sudan for seven years. Michele now resides in Florida, where she continues to minister as an author, artist, and advocate. www .illustratedgrace.com

6

Demons? Demons!

Larry Poland

One year I was asked to be a speaker for a church's youth retreat near Orlando, Florida. I arrived at the camp on a Friday afternoon and saw that there were about 120 teenagers attending. After dinner, they gathered in a rustic lodge to hear my first talk. I'd chosen to speak about the occult and the phenomenon of demon influence and possession. Then I planned to transition into the concept of surrendering to Jesus Christ and allowing His Spirit to influence and possess us to produce the power and character of Christ in our lives.

I've spoken publically thousands of times on five continents for audiences as large as twenty thousand people. I typically have no difficulty connecting words and thoughts into coherent messages. However, this Friday night was different. I couldn't keep my thoughts straight. The words just wouldn't come. And when I *finally* thought I was gaining traction with my young audience, one kid had a coughing fit, which totally distracted the group. Again, at a key point toward the end of the talk, another kid knocked a soda bottle off a bench and sent it smashing onto the concrete floor, again distracting my audience and me. I knew the talk was a disaster.

Walking away from the lodge after the session, I was met by two teen girls.

"It's really interesting that you were talking about the occult tonight," they said. "There was this new girl, Linda, on the bus ride up here who was telling us our fortunes. She was awesome! She told us stuff she could never have known about us."

All kinds of alarm bells went off in my mind. I know that demons are real. Jesus cast them out of individuals, and I'd had some encounters with them myself. That night I prayed for God's guidance. The next morning after breakfast, I called the camp leaders and counselors together for a brief meeting. "Something cultic is going on in this camp, and I think we need to be prepared and deal with it." I told them about my struggle to speak, the strange and well-timed distractions, and the fortune-telling teen on the bus. I asked them to spend some time making sure they were free of unconfessed sin, and then led them in prayer to claim victory and bind any evil spirits in the name of Jesus.

My next two talks flowed like water. There were no hesitations or distractions, and I felt complete fluency and freedom in my spirit. After the evening talk, the two girls who had told me of Linda the night before fell into step with me on the way to the campfire service. Linda was with them, and they introduced her.

"I hear you tell fortunes," I said.

"Yes, I come from three generations of fortune-tellers," Linda shared.

"What do you think about what I've been saying about being filled with the Spirit of Christ? Does that make any sense to you?"

"Yes, it does."

"Would you like to pray and invite Jesus Christ into your life to forgive your sins and fill you with His presence and power?"

"Yes," she said.

"Then, pray with me phrase by phrase as I lead you.

"Dear Lord Jesus…" I started, but Linda did not speak.

I repeated, "Dear Lord Jesus…"

Again there was silence. I opened my eyes and saw Linda convulsing. Her body was shaking and trembling from head to foot in the most violent of contortions and erratic movements. Instantly, I commanded, "In the name of Jesus, let this girl go!" Linda went limp. I thought she might fall to the ground.

I started the prayer a third time, "Dear Lord Jesus…"

Linda repeated after me the entire prayer with a weak-but-earnest voice. She was instantly delivered.

Throughout that night, I was awakened three times with an urgent sense to pray for Linda. I got out of bed and onto my knees and prayed until I felt her battle was over.

I saw Linda the next morning at breakfast and pulled her aside.

"Did you have a struggle in the night?" I asked.

She said that she had—multiple times. I told her that it would be crucial that she publically renounce her demon informers (she told me she knew their names) and openly profess her allegiance to Jesus Christ. She did so that afternoon in a sharing time with the entire camp. This sealed her freedom from bondage to the occult.

A miracle of divine power over the demonic world had occurred. There was no fancy exorcism and no complicated ecclesiastical ritual. It was simply the deployment of the supernatural power of the risen Jesus Christ through prayer.

Jesus called his twelve disciples together and gave them authority to cast out evil spirits and to heal every kind of disease and illness. (Matthew 10:1 NLT)

Excerpted from Larry W. Poland, PhD, *Miracle Walk* (Tucson: Entrust Source Publishers, 2012), pp. 16-18. Edited and used by permission.

Larry Poland is the founder and chairman of Mastermedia International and founder of the National Media Prayer Breakfast. For three decades, his organization has provided counsel on the faith community to leaders in film and television. www.master mediaintl.org.

7

Between a Rock and a Hard Place

Lee Sellick

It was a perfect summer day. Two buddies of mine, Steve and Kevin, had joined me in climbing the North Mountain in Central Oregon. We'd just finished lunch and were beginning to climb in shale and large boulders. Steve started up the ridge first, I followed about a hundred yards behind, and Kevin followed about the same distance behind me.

As I walked, the shale slid, and I gained only half a step for each step taken. Desiring to save my energy, I decided instead to hike on the rocks just ahead of me. As I came to the first boulder, I kicked it to verify that it was firmly planted. When I determined it was, I proceeded to jump onto it. As my weight shifted forward, the 2500-pound rock broke loose and began rolling—pitching me into the air backward downhill. I landed on my day pack in a fetal position and then quickly looked uphill to see which direction to move to avoid the boulder's path. Too late! A coffee-table-sized boulder hit my ankle and pinned my left leg against another boulder. I frantically tried to jerk loose, but to no avail.

As I lay with my left leg pinned down, I swiftly realized I was about to die. Any moment now, the boulder would continue rolling over my legs, over my body, and then strike its deathblow—

crushing me completely on its way down the mountain. This all seemed to occur in slow motion, as my mind processed information at the light speed. I thought, *This is really going to hurt!*

At that moment, I stuck my hand out between my legs to touch the boulder just as it reached my rear. In a loud voice I yelled, "Get that rock off of me!" The rock stopped, and then rolled six inches to the right, freeing my leg.

"That's weird," I said aloud. I immediately did a summersault downhill, away from the rock that had just pinned me. Due to the steepness of the terrain, I landed on my feet facing uphill. I was bleeding badly, so I checked to see if my injury was life-threatening. It was not. I reached down and applied pressure to stop the bleeding as Kevin arrived to assist me to a safer area. Steve arrived soon after. Steve was an amateur photographer, so he began snapping pictures. Kevin was a medical student, so he quickly assessed the damage. The boulder hit my ankle but didn't break it. It proceeded to crush the soft tissue, scraping skin off the tibia, yet it didn't break a bone. There was a deep puncture wound that a stream of blood was flowing out of, but that was stoppable.

"Did you see what happened?" I asked.

"I heard the rock break loose and start rolling," said Kevin. "I looked and saw you flying through the air headfirst downhill, looking at the sky. And then you were out of sight. I heard you yell and then nothing. I rushed to see what had happened and found you just standing, looking down at your legs."

We radioed for help, and I was picked up by a Life Flight Huey and taken to St. Charles Hospital in Bend, Oregon. I met with the emergency-room doctor, who had experienced a very similar crushing injury to the soft tissue. He was concerned I might lose my leg due to excessive swelling. To illustrate, he revealed a scar on his shin; that cut had allowed weeping so that the swelling didn't cut off his circulation. His prognosis was that I would be laid up for a minimum of four to six weeks. I would have to stay in Bend so he could assess the danger of the swelling. If it got bad, he would cut my leg open and drain it.

I asked if he'd heard that eating fresh pineapple could keep swelling down. He hadn't, so I shared that its enzymes could mitigate the risks of swelling and bruising injuries. The doctor was skeptical, so I told him I'd try it and let him know how I was doing the next day.

A friend in Bend picked me up, took me to buy a pineapple, and then hosted me for the night. I ate the entire pineapple that evening. The next day I did the same with another; the third day, I repeated the performance. Each day when the doctor called, I announced that there was no swelling or bruising. None! He didn't believe me, but after examining me he allowed me to return home to Portland. A week later, after a total of four pineapples and a lot of rest, I was able to start working again.

I see two miracles combined in this near-disastrous event: (1) that huge boulder didn't crush me because I called out to God, and (2) my quick recovery lasted only one week, instead of four or more.

I consider this a "love tap" from God to test and build my faith in adversity. God wanted me to see Him as the God of the impossible. There's no way the boulder should have stopped rolling down the mountain. However, God had already positioned an angel at my head and waited for me to call out to Him for help. When I did, the angel reached out, stopped the stone, and freed my leg.

This experience has helped teach me not to fear (as much) when difficulties arise or circumstances seem bleak. I'm more aware of what God may want me to do in His service. I know that God can and will intervene on my behalf while there is more He has for me to accomplish on this earth. Indeed, nothing can touch us if God determines that we still have work to do for Him.

He will call on me, and I will answer him; I will be with him in trouble, I will deliver him and honor him. (Psalm 91:15)

Lee Sellick owns a home-inspection business. He loves the outdoors; in fact, talking about the annual wilderness adventure race that he helped develop gets him wildly excited. He and his wife have two grown children and a daughter-in-law.

8

No Weapon

ANTOINE McCOY

The tornado-warning sirens were blasting as I approached the road that led to the school where I teach in a small city in Madison County, Alabama. When I entered the building, all the children were on their knees, facing the wall, holding their hands above their heads. This was the tornado drill position we'd regularly practiced during the school year. *Just another practice, right?* I thought. I wasn't surprised or concerned in the least. Yet as two more hours crept by, the sirens went off three more times. The decision was made to follow tornado drill procedures and bus the children home.

Two more hours later and still unconcerned, I was finally cleared to leave the school. During the forty-five-minute drive home across the county, the sun was shining and the roads were peaceful and practically empty. Subdivisions were intact, the local gas station had a few cars pumping gas, and people were at the local Piggly Wiggly buying supplies for the severe thunderstorm that had been forecast.

I thought to myself, *What a waste of gas to drive across the county and back home just for a severe thunderstorm and tornado warning.*

I'm from New York City. I've been in snowstorms and blizzards.

They just need to lighten up down here in the South, I thought dismissively.

Upon arriving home, I found that the power was out. Still I wasn't concerned. It was broad daylight. My wife, Melissa, was also home early from work and peacefully taking a nap.

It wasn't until I turned on my battery-powered MP3 player to listen to the local radio station that I first felt a stab of fear. According to the reports, a tornado had just touched down in a neighboring county and was heading toward Madison. I woke up Melissa and told her about the warning. She was eight months pregnant with our first child and noticeably shaken up as she held her belly and looked to me for comfort and direction. While I didn't feel prepared to protect anyone, I immediately found a flashlight, blankets, and pillows and placed them in an empty closet. This was the safest place I could think of for taking immediate cover.

The radio was now reporting that the tornado had entered Madison County and that it would be in our town in a few minutes.

"Find shelter!" said the speaker.

This storm is real, I thought. I don't know what prompted me to do what I did next, but I did what one is never supposed to do in the face of an impending tornado and thunderstorm: I went to the front door and looked outside. The clouds were becoming gray and overcast, but, strangely, the air was still quiet and calm.

My wife broke the silence. "Do you hear that?"

I strained to listen but heard nothing.

"Do you hear that sound?" she asked.

Again, I tried to focus my attention. Then I heard it. "It sounds like a train," I said.

She immediately pulled me inside and said, "That's a tornado on the ground coming our way!"

We ran to the shelter of our closet. I may have been unprepared and surprised in every other way, but now I knew there was a weapon that was stronger than any preparation or foreknowledge I could have had. Without hesitation, I grabbed my wife's hand and began to pray with all that was within me.

Lord, please protect Melissa, the baby, and me. Protect our neighbors and our neighborhood from the storm. You are God of the universe. You have the power to lift tornados over our house and neighborhood. You promised in Isaiah 54:17 that no weapon formed against us would prosper and in Psalm 91 that you would command your angels to guard us in all our ways. Send your angels now and protect us. In Jesus' name, amen.

With that short prayer, I held my wife's hand tightly and tried to comfort her. Now we had to wait. The wind was roaring. Our house began to shake and rock lightly back and forth. While I was feeling absolutely terrified, I continued repeating those verses under my breath and praying that the windows of our house wouldn't break. The violent wind alone could cause major damage and be a great danger to us.

Five minutes later, it was all over. The tornado had passed, and everything was calm. Melissa and I crawled out of the closet and thanked God together for protecting us and our home. Fifteen minutes later, our neighbor from across the road knocked on our door and asked how we were doing. I told him we were shaken up, but thankfully no one was hurt. I saw that my yard had a few broken branches and some debris in it, but the damage was nothing compared to what the meteorologists on the radio had told us to expect.

My neighbor, however, was trembling. When I asked him what was wrong, he pulled out his smartphone and started showing me pictures. What I saw made my stomach drop. The Piggly Wiggly and gas station that I had driven by less than an hour ago were completely demolished. The houses in a subdivision only half a mile away were totally destroyed. Homes in the neighborhood next to ours were in shambles, and trees were strewn everywhere. Yet our home and the houses in our subdivision and neighborhood were standing without any substantial damage.

Melissa and I were speechless. God answered our prayers for protection not only for our own home, but also for our entire neighborhood. In the aftermath of the tornado outbreak, we learned that the tornados that had swept through our area were some of the deadliest ever recorded in the history of the United States. They were classified as EF5, the highest-ranking possible for these kinds of twisters. And they had touched down that day in Madison County.

Our community experienced tragedy that day that cannot be explained, but I do know this to be true: One small, quick prayer of faith is a powerful weapon because we pray to a powerful God. Though we were unprepared, out of His own goodness and sovereignty God more than protected us when we called on His name.

No weapon that is formed against you will prosper. (Isaiah 54:17 NASB)

Antoine McCoy is a National Board Certified K-12 teacher who is passionate about helping adults and kids discover their God-given passions. http://antoinemccoy.com.

9

Anna's Answer

David Sanford

"**D**oes God speak to us today?" This is a question that has been debated for centuries. Two of my beloved mentors have insisted for more than thirty-five years that the Lord doesn't speak to anyone—*ever*. Sure, God spoke in ancient times to biblical prophets, but according to them, He stopped before the close of the first century AD.

But I remember the first time the Lord spoke to me. It was at the end of an intensive time of prayer. He was quiet, yet crystal clear. I didn't know what to do, so I grabbed a pen and recorded in detail what He told me. Since that experience, my struggle hasn't been with whether God *does* speak today; my struggle has been with the thousands of times He chooses not to say a word.

This struggle was certainly true in the early days of the Great Recession in 2007. My wife and I were still recovering from severe business losses. Clients had canceled five large media projects midstream, and some refused to honor contractual terms. In short, we were left with zero income.

At the same time our eldest son, Jonathan, was to be married in San Luis Obispo, California—nine hundred miles away from our home. My wife, Renée, and I did the math. It would cost at least $1800 for the four of us—Renée, our son Benjamin, our daughter, Anna, and me—to travel to the wedding, pay for the rehearsal dinner, and then travel home. It didn't even look like we had the money to even show up. As a husband and father, I can't begin to tell you how helpless and hopeless I felt.

The four of us agreed to pray for $2000 "just in case" and, as always, decided to tell no one of our situation except God. Within a week, we received an anonymous gift for $1000. Renée, Benjamin, and Anna were thrilled. I felt smaller than ever. *Sure, we could get to the wedding and pay for part of the rehearsal dinner, but what then?* I was depressed beyond words.

Sensing my downcast state, my ten-year-old daughter tried to cheer me up. "Hey, Dad, do you think that $1000 came because *you* were praying? No, it was me! Don't worry about anything. God is going to provide."

She paused.

I didn't smile.

"In fact," Anna continued, "I want you to make a deal with me. You don't pray—just me. And you don't get the mail either. Only I can get it. Promise?"

I didn't respond.

"Promise?"

"Okay." I turned to hide the expressions of grief and anger now racing across my face. Our trip was slated to start the following Wednesday morning. *What kind of father can't afford to go to his eldest son's wedding?*

The next afternoon, Anna came running through the door and said, "Dad, guess what? The check didn't come in the mail today. That means it *has* to come tomorrow, Saturday, Monday, or Tuesday. Isn't that exciting, Dad?"

"Anna, darling, another check isn't coming," I said. "I don't know why, but God sent only $1000. That's all we're getting."

Anna smiled. "That's why you're not praying and not getting the mail, Dad!"

After school the next day, Anna came skipping into the house with the mail. She was almost giddy. "Dad, you're not going to believe it! The check didn't come in the mail today. That means it *has* to come tomorrow, Monday, or Tuesday. Can you believe it?"

No, I can't believe I'm in this situation, I thought. *I can't believe I can't afford to go to my own son's wedding.* I felt worse than ever.

Saturday was terrible. When the mailman came, Anna rushed out of the sliding-glass door, over to the gate, and up to his truck. He handed her our mail for the day. Anna was bobbing up and down when she came back into the house. I'd rarely seen her so excited. "Dad, I can't believe it! The check didn't come in the mail today. That means it *has* to come Monday or Tuesday." She couldn't contain her enthusiasm.

I couldn't contain my anguish, so I quickly turned and walked away. *How can I get her to understand?* I wondered. *God doesn't always give us what* we think *we need. Even here in America, Christians often go through much worse things than this. Still, I'm so embarrassed and so ashamed. I'm such a failure.*

I didn't have a good morning at church. I felt completely dry, empty, and hollow. I knew this feeling from one of my worst moments mountain climbing. I felt as if I were hanging by one hand onto the edge of a precipice with no rope and more than 400 feet of air between me and the ground below.

I honestly couldn't pray. *Why even try?* I thought.

After school on Monday, Anna ran through the front door almost yelling. "Dad, this is so exciting! The check didn't come in the mail today. That means it *has* to come tomorrow!" She was literally jumping up and down.

"Anna, you don't understand. I don't know what we're going to do, but no check is coming. We have the $1000. That's it. That's all we're getting."

Anna just smiled. "I told you, Dad. It's not your prayers. It's mine."

Sure enough, Tuesday afternoon Anna ran into the house, jumping higher than ever. "Dad," she practically yelled, "this is so exciting! The check *didn't* come in the mail. That means someone is going to knock on our front door in five minutes and hand it to us."

"That's never going to happen!" I snapped.

"But God told me."

"God didn't tell you that!" I yelled. I was furious. I couldn't bear the inescapable shame that lay ahead of me.

A few minutes later, when I had started to cool off, I heard the doorbell. I yelled again (but more politely) for Anna to take care of it. Thirty seconds later she flew into the kitchen with the biggest brown eyes possible. In her hands she held an envelope.

"Pastor Jim just came to our door. He can't say who, but somebody came by his office and said, 'God impressed upon me that David and Renée Sanford's family needs help. I feel it's urgent. You'll see they get this within the hour, won't you?' "

I couldn't hold back the tears. "I am so sorry, Anna. I said terrible things. I said God didn't speak to you. He really did. Will you forgive me?"

I'll never forget how hard she hugged me. After a minute she whispered into my ear, "I told you it was *my* prayers." I laughed hard for the first time in weeks.

Then Anna handed me a check signed by the senior pastor of Spring Mountain Bible Church in the amount of $1000.

Later, I thought about my oldest mentor who had recently gone to be with the Lord. Yes, we're all in for a lot of surprises when we get to heaven. He now knows, beyond question, that God can speak to anyone, anytime, and in such a crystal-clear way that there's no other option except to acknowledge that it is Him. Thanks to His incredible sovereignty, providence, holiness, love, and mystery, you and I can stop telling God what He can and cannot do.

My God will meet all your needs according to the riches of his glory in Christ Jesus. (Philippians 4:19)

David Sanford serves on the leadership team at Corban University (www.corban.edu). He works with leaders in the busy intersection of public speaking, social networking, mass media interviewing, and book publishing. David and Renée have been married for more than thirty-three years. They have five children and eleven grandchildren (including one in heaven).

10

Consider It Joy

RHONDA S.

When my two children were in elementary school, my prayers for them were simple. I prayed for them to do well in school, to have fun, to stay safe, and to make and be good friends. As they grew up, my prayers gradually changed. I mistakenly assumed that prayers could be the same for both my children—that what worked for one child would work for the other.

When my son, the younger of the two, was a senior in high school, my prayers contained obvious requests like God's direction for his future, teacher–student relationships, deep friendships, and preparation for college, but they were intermingled with prayers for his personal safety and deliverance from drugs and alcohol.

This precious boy of mine had always been very sweet and sensitive. He was the one who would enjoy "mommy time" by cuddling with me any chance he had. He appeared to have a different personality than his sibling, but that was how God was molding and shaping him. I actually thought he would be the easier of the two to discipline and raise.

What I didn't know was that by his senior year, he'd been smoking marijuana for over three years. Some of his friendships were compromising his safety, and he had dabbled in other drugs. I guess the transformation really began once he entered high school. He was a bright, funny, and very kind young man going into his freshman year. I believe that year he began looking for the approval of his peers and doing whatever it took to receive it. Unfortunately, as parents, we gave way too many excuses for the changes in his behavior and attitude. With each passing year, we drifted further and further apart in our relationship.

As his senior year progressed and I realized graduation was approaching, I was certain the Lord would answer my prayers by having him attend the Christian college he'd been accepted to. I believed he needed new friends, a new atmosphere, and a fresh start. However, his bad choices continued. With very heavy hearts, we decided he would attend a local state university.

Everything came to a head two weeks before he was to leave. My husband and I didn't realize just how hard the devil was attacking our entire family. We seemed to be falling apart as individuals and as a whole. To this day I can still hear the yelling and feel the sting of tears. We'd made a written agreement that he would not have any drug paraphernalia in our home. I had run out to do a couple errands, and when I returned I couldn't believe how heavily our home smelled of marijuana. Then I knew what needed to be done, but I was heartbroken about having to do it. I asked him to leave our home per our signed agreement.

The next thirty minutes were horrific. He proceeded to call me every name in the book, to tear me down as an individual, as a mom, and as a Christian with his words. Everything he did was to hurt and infuriate me.

I was much calmer than I thought I could be. With every stab to my heart, I reached for God's comfort. At one point I had tears in my eyes, but I wasn't overly emotional. As he grabbed a backpack and headed for the door, the thought crossed my mind that, for what felt like the first time, I wouldn't have any idea where he was going, who he would be with, or what he would be doing. I watched my son take his skateboard and ride down our driveway until he was out of sight. The pain was almost unbearable. Even with all the questions whirling around in my head, in that very moment I heard God's still, small voice say, "I love him more than you do."

In that moment, I knew something had to change. I didn't know exactly how, but that didn't matter. My prayer life and devotions would have to be transformed. Instead of praying for my son's circumstances, I began praying for the way I would handle them. My life verse immediately became James 1:2-3—that regardless of my situation and all the heartbreak, I agreed to "count it pure joy" and wholeheartedly give my son back to God, no matter what that looked like. It was a transformation toward knowing the peace of God, which truly does pass all understanding. While there were still tears and times of sadness, they were fewer and further between. I had hope for my life and the life of my son.

He was gone seven days before he returned home. Although his recreational life using drugs didn't change, he was willing to conform to our new rules and go to college. The next two years of college, he continued getting high. He functioned adequately in family settings when he needed to, acting somewhat appropriately during the holidays and when he came home to be in his sister's wedding. I continued to wholeheartedly pray for him and believe in God's plan for his life.

During the summer between his sophomore and junior years of college, he was offered a job. We were so excited for him, believing it would help him gain responsibility and maturity. Unfortunately, it turned out to be an environment filled with people who were also using drugs. We knew he'd still been using his drug of choice—marijuana—but now he was beginning to dabble more in others. Praying my son through each day became a normal way of life. His life was out of my hands; only God could take care of him now.

I didn't think life could get worse than the first time he skateboarded out of our lives. I was wrong. The second time he left was the worst day of my entire life. The words that came out of my son's mouth broke my heart into pieces. Yet to my surprise, I remained calm and controlled. I remember sensing it was the influence of the drugs talking and not my son. Before he left, God's still small voice again spoke to me and gently led me to share with him some very powerful words.

I told him that from that very second, all the filth that was vomited out of his mouth toward me was already forgiven. I told him there was nothing he could ever say or do that would change my unconditional love for him. I had no idea what the future held for us at that moment, but because of the words I was sharing, I knew God was in control and I was not.

And then, for the second time, I watched him leave our driveway once again, this time in a car. With this departure, I felt physically ill. I fell onto our driveway, sobbing uncontrollably and gasping for air. The pain in my heart was absolutely excruciating.

He was gone for only a few days. When he returned, we made it very clear that since we'd already been down this road, things would be quite different going forward. The first difference was that he was required to meet with a man who had experience helping addicts. The second difference was that if he didn't keep up with his end of the bargain, we would finally follow through on previous idle threats by providing no funding for college, cutting off any and all financial help, and asking him to move out of our home.

After approximately three months, our son became completely drug free. This was by his choice and in his timing!

Before this trial, I was striving for a pain-free life. I clung to my family as if they were my own. I had yet to wholeheartedly give them to Jesus. Without this trial, I would not have known the constant communion of God, who is our faithful Father, who takes care of my children whenever and wherever they are, and who supplied me with everything I needed as a mother.

The change in our son has been so extreme that friends and family often make comments after spending time with him. He is once again respectful, helpful, and a joy to be around. He often offers us information about his whereabouts and the people he will be with. God has ahold of him and is working in and through him. I trust that He will never let go.

One day, nearing the end of my son's junior year in college, I drove up our driveway to the place where I'd fallen on my face in anguish the second time he had left our home. In that very moment, I received a text from him letting me know that he had just read an excerpt from a devotional book I sent him. He went on to explain how God had provided just what he needed through those words that day.

Pure joy.

Consider it pure joy, my brothers and sisters, whenever you face trials of many kinds, because you know that the testing of your faith produces perseverance. (James 1:2-3)

Rhonda S. was a stay-at-home mom for twenty years, and loves doing volunteer work with children and teaching Sunday school. She has also enjoyed leading a Moms in Prayer group for more than fifteen years. Rhonda and her husband have two grown children, one son-in-love, and two precious grandchildren.

11

Feast or Famine

Suzanne Frey

If you and I had known each other when I was in college, at any given time I would have probably been on a diet. I was *always* on a diet. I was not obese, but my roommate called me "thunder thighs." I was definitely overweight. I remember many mornings waking up and looking for something to wear that would fit my chunky body, wishing it would be socially acceptable to wear my bathrobe all day.

If I wasn't on a diet, I was binge eating everything I'd deprived myself of while dieting. I would start at Baskin-Robbins, ordering a brownie hot-fudge sundae. Then I'd go to the local donut shop for a large apple fritter and a chocolate-glazed donut. After that it was back home to make and consume a large batch of chocolate chip cookies. All of this would take place within a few hours. I'd be so stuffed I could hardly walk. This feast-or-famine cycle was very normal for me. It was the way I dealt with life. It was the way I handled feelings of loneliness, rejection, fear, and anger. Anytime I felt sad or when something didn't work out the way I wanted it to, I went to food for comfort.

Blaise Pascal, a French philosopher, said, "There is a God-shaped vacuum in the heart of every person, which cannot be filled by any created thing, but only by God, the Creator, made known through Jesus Christ." Even though I was raised in a supportive family that went to church every Sunday, I always thought God was "way up there" and that I was "way down here," alone in my struggles. It wasn't until my freshman year of college that someone told me I could know God personally through Jesus Christ—that He wanted to be my friend. I didn't have to feel like He was "way up there." He wanted to give me life now and every day, not just when I went to church. At eighteen years old, I asked Him to be my Lord and Savior, to forgive and cleanse me from all the things I had done wrong, and to make me a new person.

It wasn't as if the next day I suddenly lost all desire for food, but God began working in my heart and life. I started reading the Bible and understanding that God loved me unconditionally whether I was fat or thin or on a diet or binge day. What I weighed on the scale was a much bigger issue to me than it was to Him. Yes, He cared and wanted me to have victory. My overeating was an outward sign of something that was wrong on the inside. I didn't feel good about who I was. If someone were to ask me to describe myself in three words, I would have said "insecure, unimportant, inadequate." Only God was capable of changing my view of myself.

He began showing me in His Word that He loved me. I started to realize that because I was made in His image, I was beautiful and precious in His sight. Reading through the life of Jesus, I understood more fully that God wanted to deliver me from this bondage. But I still felt the pull of my old habits dragging me down. I would make promises to God, put myself on more diets and programs, and even vow to fast for as many days as I could, thinking that if Jesus fasted forty days, so could I. Oh, and I'd drop several pounds while I was at it. But when my promises didn't last, I felt I let God down.

I was desperate to be free. I longed to be normal and see food not as my purpose for living but as fuel to help me live life with purpose. I was a prisoner, and it seemed that the harder I tried to be good and eat well, the harder I fell back into binging and depression. I was depressed because I ate too much, and even more depressed because I gained another two or three pounds when I did so. It was a crazy cycle. By the time I graduated from college, I was forty pounds overweight.

I related to Paul's words: "I don't really understand myself, for I want to do what is right, but I don't do it. Instead, I do what I hate…Who will free me from this life that is dominated by sin and death?" (Romans 7:15, 24 NLT).

Paul gives the answer: live according to the Spirit of Jesus (Romans 8). I realized that the same power that raised Jesus from the dead also lived in me. Therefore, I could triumph. I put two requests before God: (1) *Help me relearn how to feed my stomach only when it is truly hungry and to stop eating when I am satisfied,* and (2) *help me learn how to feed my heart through a living relationship with You.*

I identified that my overwhelming passion for food wasn't caused by physical hunger but by a temptation from the enemy, who was trying to keep me idolizing it. So in those moments when hunger hit, I went directly to God by opening my Bible and getting on my knees in prayer. The Lord gave me a passion for His presence. I began experiencing the fullness of God, something I could truly delight in.

Food and eating are obviously not bad things. In fact, they are great things. Not only are food and eating necessary to live, but they are also gifts from God to be enjoyed. But food had become my idol. God provides food to fill empty stomachs, not empty hearts.

It was God alone who answered my prayers. *He changed me.* It happened over time, though, through one small choice after another. He led me to realize that temptation was not worth saying yes to, and gave me His power and strength to say no. My small choices eventually became new habits, which became new behaviors. His Spirit released me, healed me, and made me whole. He filled the empty hole in my heart that I'd been stuffing with food.

All that time I'd been famished for God! When I began feasting on His Word and presence, I experienced even more freedom.

After college, I lost the extra forty pounds, reached a healthy weight, and began feeling confident in my body. I began making healthy choices and have continued to do so up to this day—nearly thirty years later. I'm in no way perfect. I still sin. But by God's grace, I no longer have this struggle with food. I no longer binge or live in fear of putting myself on a diet tomorrow. God completely set me free from a life controlled by food.

This is more than just a weight-loss story. This is a story of how God took an overweight, insecure, and very average eighteen-year-old young woman and made her into a new creation. He broke the chains the devil had bound me with and launched me to liberty. Satan wanted to destroy me: "The thief comes only to steal and kill and destroy." But Jesus said: "I have come that they may have life, and have it to the full" (John 10:10).

Satan wanted to lead me to a place of staying fat and sad. God's destiny for me was to be healthy and whole. He heard my years of crying for deliverance! Today I am no longer in that prison. I am truly free.

[The Lord said to me,] "My grace is all you need. My power works best in weakness." So now I am glad to boast about my weaknesses, so that the power of Christ can work through me. (2 Corinthians 12:9 NLT)

Suzanne Frey has been a business owner and manager for more than twenty years. She's actively involved with Moms in Prayer, and is a member of Toastmasters International. Suzanne and her husband, Ron, live in Oregon and have three grown children.

12

Bullet-Stopping Prayer

Jim M.

*B*rrring, brrring. The phone rang out at 1:14 AM Sunday morning. "Your son has been gravely injured," an unknown voice said on the line. "We need your medical insurance information before we can transport him to the hospital."

Our fun-loving son, Jay, had traveled to the mountains in Colorado with some friends. My wife, Julie, and I didn't have a good feeling about the trip or the friends he was going with—and neither did Jay. Our daughter even had misgivings about it. At the last minute, however, he decided to go.

Later we heard more of the story. Jay and his friends heard a deer moving above their campground, so they went to have a look. Jay was carrying a .22-caliber handgun. Why his friend brought it along, we don't know. Whether they saw a deer or not, we don't know. What we do know is that Jay slipped and dropped the gun, and it fired.

Jay didn't immediately realize he'd shot himself, but he did feel a shock go through his body. The slug entered his groin, missing the main artery by the narrowest of margins. If it had severed that artery, he would have bled out and died before he could have reached help.

The long, bumpy ride out of the campsite to the main road was torturous. Upon reaching that road, the boys realized they were a long way from anywhere. Fortunately, there was an emergency phone by the roadside from which they called for help.

When help came, they called us. It was a frightening wake-up call. I gave them the medical insurance information, and they told me they would transport Jay to the local rural hospital, forty-five minutes away. No good thoughts were going through our heads. Once Jay was at the hospital, I contacted the emergency physician on my cell phone, asking for Jay to be transferred to Denver where I knew he would receive better care.

"We don't have time," the physician said. "We need to do a workup and operate immediately or we might lose him."

My wife and I jumped into our car. The two-and-a-half-hour drive into the mountains was a horrible ride fraught with terrible thoughts of losing our son. After a while, Julie said, "Please stop talking about it. I can't take any more." We arrived at the hospital just as they wheeled Jay out of the operating room. He was alive and would surely make it. The road back would be long, but there was a road back.

Once we knew Jay was going to be all right, we had to call our daughter, Jessica, and let her know what happened. At the time she was on a mission trip in India, and the team had very strict rules that parents were not to call unless it was a dire emergency. We found the phone number and placed a call to India.

One of the counselors answered, and I nervously explained that we indeed had a family emergency. He called in Jessica. I will never forget her first words to me.

Crying, she blurted out, "Is Jay dead?"

I was shocked.

She went on to relate that earlier that week she'd had a feeling Jay was going to die. She'd asked members of her team to pray for him.

What a joyous report I could give to Jay's sister! "No, Jessica, Jay is not dead. He is alive! He was shot, but the bullet just missed the artery."

"Dad," she replied, "it was our prayers and the hand of God that stayed the bullet."

Behold, I am the Lord, the God of all flesh; is anything too difficult for Me? (Jeremiah 32:27 NASB)

Jim M. is a corporate executive and enjoys long-distance biking, hiking, and golf.

13

The Last Assignment

JOHN WARTON

Mine was not a foxhole conversion. In fact, it was just the opposite. It was 1969. Our mission was to fly along the southern Vietnam–Cambodia border to watch for soldiers and materiel from the north entering through Cambodia. Our Huey (military helicopter) had two pilots, two gunners, and one mission commander (me). Two gun ships supported us below, and a troop transport was flying with us. Once we observed enemy activity, we would deploy our assets as needed. It was one o'clock in the morning, and we had just refueled after our first two-hour patrol. We were ready to take off for another.

I'd flown this mission many times over the past couple of months, qualifying for an air medal. I'd already served four months at a regional headquarters, another four months with a Special Forces advisory team fighting with two battalions of national soldiers, and now a border-surveillance and combat-support mission.

My tour had been remarkably safe, despite combat engagements and other soldiers being killed around me. I didn't have many days left in my tour. In fact, I shouldn't have even been flying that night; I was due to leave in the morning for a week's R and R in Bangkok. And yet there I was, commanding another surveillance flight.

The first two hours were uneventful. At high altitude, we'd spotted some convoys near the Cambodian capital, Phnom Penh, turning east after completing the long drive south from Hanoi. It would be daylight before they reached the Vietnam border. Our fuel started running low, so we returned to our airfield base to refuel. As we lifted off, we realized something had been improperly set in the cockpit during that stop, and the Huey had insufficient power to sustain flight. At barely a hundred feet above the ground, a blaring siren went off in the headphones my team was wearing. The Huey shuddered and then began to wobble. We pitched back and forth, and then our descent went out of control. Instead of whirling at 6600 RPMs, the blades were spinning at only 5800 RPMs. At 5600 RPMs, the Huey stops flying.

I instantly realized the danger of our situation. We'd just refueled and were carrying flares and explosives. Any minute now, we could explode in a gigantic ball of flames upon impact. As I realized I was about to die, I clutched the metal frame of my seat. My entire life flashed through my mind in what seemed like fast-forward scenes: grade school, my dog, our house, prom, and my fiancée. And then I prayed, *Jesus, save me.*

I am sure it was an inaudible prayer; I think it was the "groaning too deep to be uttered" (Romans 8). It was, however, a deep and sincere prayer directed to Jesus. I grew up attending a traditional church and had heard many passages from the Bible. But when I left for Vietnam, my fiancée's parents had urged me to read the Bible for myself. I bought a paperback edition of the Bible to carry with me, and I'd read it throughout the entire year. It was wonderful. It filled me with comforting and encouraging words of truth. It gave me broad perspectives that I'd never entertained before, even when I was in college. The Bible also filled me with convicting words about some of my conduct and attitudes.

In that moment in the descending Huey, almost instinctively my heart cried out to Jesus: "Save me!" And immediately I saw Him. He was dressed in dazzling white robes, as He was in the transfiguration. He was seated as if on a tribunal, like the Lincoln Monument in Washington, DC. Suddenly the Huey stabilized and hovered steadily, without vibration, just above the treetops.

After several seconds in this position, the pilots felt confident to continue and began an upward ascent away from the base. We hadn't flown fifteen seconds before the same blaring signal rang again in the headphones. We were shuddering, vibrating, pitching, dropping. This time, however, I sat calmly with my arms folded in my lap. No further prayer. No conscious trusting for rescue from the crash. Yet no fear and no anxiety. Again, just above the trees, the pilots were able to stabilize the Huey. A few moments later, we landed. Everyone ran away from the aircraft. We didn't return to the mission that night.

It was my last time in a combat operation. I left for my R and R a few hours later, and then I was off to headquarters with my gear for a return to the United States. President Nixon's reduction in force meant an early return home for me.

In those final moments of combat in Vietnam, the God of the Bible revealed Himself to me. He was not just a figure of ancient history, much less of religious fable. He was very real. He was accessible at a heart's cry. He was aware of my situation and more than able to intervene.

I hadn't survived a year's tour in Vietnam because I was careful, smart, or even lucky. No, it was God who protected me through it all. It seemed incredible that Jesus could stop a Huey from crashing, but I had just experienced it. What was even more perplexing was why He answered my prayer and saved me. I was in no way worthy of His intervention; I wasn't even a churchgoer or a particularly moral or noble man. *Why me?*

Over the next few days, I pored over the Bible I'd read the past year. Now, however, I knew it all was true: Jesus was real, and He had died when I had not. He had been raised from the dead, and I too was alive even though I should have died. Then I found 1 Corinthians 15:3-4: "Christ died for our sins according to the

Scriptures…he was buried…[and] he was raised on the third day according to the Scriptures."

That was why He died—for my sins! And He had returned to life as I had experienced Him that night as the Huey was falling through the air. Four days later, I confessed to the living Savior my sinful pride, arrogance, and lust—all of which, I realized, He already knew about. I put my trust for forgiveness and cleansing in Him. Ever since that time, I have been able to say in more than one way, "Jesus saved me!"

What I received I passed on to you as of first importance: that Christ died for our sins according to the Scriptures, that he was buried, that he was raised on the third day according to the Scriptures. (1 Corinthians 15:3-4)

John Warton served five years in the US Army. Following language school and special warfare training, he was sent to Vietnam in 1969. After his tours of duty, John married and entered business in Chicago. He and his wife have four children and twelve grandchildren.

14

Squeezed by a Lemon

Kimberly Moxley

I had a vision of my perfect car. It wasn't a spiritual vision where the heavens opened up and I heard the audible voice of God. Rather, it was the less-than-heavenly vision of my young, naïve, college-student self with some grand ideas about what car she should be driving.

I dreamed of an SUV. I'd worked my way through college, riding the metro for three years to my bank job and paying for school out of my own pocket semester by semester. Now I was months away from graduating with a bachelor's degree completely debt free. My parents were three thousand miles away, so I was on my own for this first car-buying experience.

I thought an SUV was cute. Plus, it was big. My train of thought was, *The bigger, the safer.* I set out with a friend to shop for cars, and soon we found ourselves at a used-car dealership. The salespeople were all smiles as they led me to a lovely looking purple Suzuki SUV with a fancy letter *S* on the hood. I couldn't even tell you the model. I just remember thinking it was perfect. Not waiting another second, I signed all the paperwork right there on the spot. I gave them $16,000 of money that I'd borrowed, and they gave me the keys.

"Isn't it great that you can just sign your name and drive away with something as nice as *this*?" I said to my friend as we pulled out of the lot. But I couldn't shake a weird feeling of apprehension.

Sure enough, the next morning I started the car and a big plume of black smoke came out of the tailpipe. After three more black plumes within an hour of just driving to and from the store, I decided to seek counsel. I talked to a friend who told me to take it in for an oil change. When I did, I got news that made me sick.

"Um, ma'am," said the mechanic, "this car probably has eighty thousand miles on it. I don't think the oil has ever been changed since it drove off the lot as a brand-new car."

He continued. "See this pink hue that is showing on my fingers? That shows the engine is full of corrosion. Whoever owned this car before you ran it into the ground. This is on its last legs."

I tried to take the car back. Needless to say, they wouldn't let me. They had just made $16,000 from a lemon, and they were gloating and quoting back to me the fine print of their paperwork that I'd missed in my over-zealous signing. The reality of what I'd just done came crashing in. I went back to my dorm room and wept in embarrassment and the lack of wisdom on my part. Two days prior, I was debt free. This lemon would take at least five years to pay off, at the end of which I would still need a good car. I felt like I'd made one horrible decision, something I'd done of my own will without seeking God's wisdom and counsel. I'd erased everything I'd accomplished. What a fool I had been.

To add to the stress of this poor financial choice, I'd been working hard in my job. I was making high sales numbers and doing everything to the best of my ability, but I hadn't received a raise in two years. I realized that I would now need another job to buy a second car. And even then, I wasn't sure if I would be approved for another loan because my credit was new and still being established.

I remember not eating much that week. I cried out to God, repenting for my foolishness and asking for forgiveness. I asked

Him to deliver me from my own naïveté and to somehow, in His mighty wisdom, get me out of this mess. The car dealership knew exactly what they were doing when they sold me the SUV, and for the first time in my life, I truly felt as if I'd encountered wickedness.

But then I was reminded that God is bigger than any devious plans of wicked men. Through my sorrow over my poor decision, God reminded me of the many little financial miracles He'd done for me in the five years I had been supporting myself. He had directed my steps before in this area, and I felt Him challenging me to trust Him again. The day I was finally able to lay this mistake at His feet and let go of the heartache, I got a call from the dealership telling me that the company they had hoped would finance me said they would not because my credit was too new. Apparently, I needed to be making at least twenty-five cents more an hour before they would even consider loaning me the money.

In other words, I needed to return my SUV.

"I'll bring it back today," I said and hung up the phone. I had never been so relieved!

Then it got even crazier. Exactly one week later, I received a two-dollar-an-hour raise in my job. I knew then God had been protecting me all along.

Soon afterward, a friend introduced me to the son of a man who owned a major car dealership in my town. I knew him because he came into my bank's branch on a daily basis to make the dealership's deposits. He found me a car that was previously owned by a grandma and grandpa; apparently they had only used it when they needed a second car, which wasn't very often. It only had 47,000 miles on it, and it was six years old. It looked brand-new. It wasn't the SUV I'd envisioned, but it was what God knew I needed. I'm still driving it today, ten years after the ordeal, and it's going strong. And best of all, I paid it off in three years! And that terrible dealership who sold me the lemon? Their practices eventually caught up to them, and they went out of business.

Keep your life free from love of money, and be content with what you have, for he has said, "I will never leave you nor forsake you." So we can confidently say, "The Lord is my helper; I will not fear; what can man do to me?" (Hebrews 13:5-6 ESV)

Kimberly Moxley has a Bachelors of Church Music degree and recently left her job as a music engraver to be a stay-at-home mom.

15

That Was God

DAYLE LUM

God has given me much in my life, including my husband, Andy. He is a godly man, loving husband, and great dad to our four children. He was a successful doctor who also took good care of his health and practiced what he preached. On a bright Sunday morning in January, Andy, Tommy (the youngest of our four children), and I drove to church singing "Blessed Be Your Name," by Matt Redman, which talks about how God gives and takes away.

After church, Andy mentioned to Tommy that he felt dizzy. A few minutes later, Andy fell. Tommy called to me from the kitchen saying something was wrong. Andy told me to take his blood pressure. I took it three times, and each time it was escalating. We rushed him to the ER.

The next seven hours were the hardest in my life. The doctors took a CT scan of Andy's brain, and they could tell he'd suffered a cerebral hemorrhage, which is a kind of brain aneurysm. The next thing I knew, Andy was in surgery to stop the bleeding. We weren't sure if he would survive.

And so began a string of miracles. Tommy and I called the family to come to the hospital in Portland, Oregon. Our eldest son Joshua and his wife drove in from Washington; our daughter

Anna took the next flight out from San Diego; and our daughter Sarah was miraculously able to leave her research in Belize and fly home. Many people in our church family and my Moms in Prayer group came to the hospital. By 9:30 that night, there were about forty of us in the surgical waiting room praying for Andy. When the neurosurgeon came out, he said that Andy had suffered a second brain aneurysm. The bleeding had somehow stopped, and the doctor was unsure why.

That was God, I thought.

Andy was in a drug-induced coma for the next three weeks to keep his body still while his brain was healing. During that time, we sent out numerous emergency prayer requests for Andy. His blood pressure, temperature, and cerebral pressures often spiked into dangerous zones because the part of his brain that regulates those things was impaired.

Even amid the turmoil I could see our loving heavenly Father watching the hearts of His children and hearing all our prayer requests for Andy. I saw Him saying, "Yes, yes, yes," to each request. Time and again, after the prayer warriors prayed, Andy's blood pressure, temperature, and cerebral pressures came down to normal levels.

The doctors frequently had to take Andy's blood to see how he was doing. One day a tech couldn't find a vein after inserting the needle a couple of times. With all the poking Andy had undergone during his time in the hospital, it had become increasingly hard to find good ones. When the tech left the room, I put out a text message prayer request that the tech would be able to find a good vein. When he returned, he immediately found a good one and was successful in getting a sample.

That was God, I thought.

Toward the end of the three weeks, the doctors took Andy off the drugs and began to bring him out of his induced coma.

I was in a daze. Everything in my life had turned upside down. I asked God to help me on this journey. On Sunday, January 29, a double rainbow appeared in the sky—just as there had been on the day Andy and I got married.

God is true to His promises, I thought. *This looks to be a good start of the day*. And sure enough, that very morning at 8:03, Andy moved his right leg and right toes. I called the nurse, and she witnessed it too. This was the first time Andy had moved. He was starting to wake up from the coma.

There are three things in life that Andy has always kept constant: his faith in Jesus Christ, his love for me, and his sense of humor. That night, when our daughter Sarah was saying good night to Andy, she kissed him—and he puckered up for another kiss. When she said, "Mom will be here in the morning," he smiled.

Soon afterward, a respiratory tech capped Andy's trachea for a little while so he could speak. The first thing Andy said to me when he woke up was, "I love you." God knew I needed that. During our twenty-seven years of marriage, Andy has said, "I love you" to me every day.

As Andy's vitals seemed to be stabilizing, one of the resident doctors in the progressive care unit (PCU) suggested he be sent to a skilled nursing facility as his next step toward recovery. I felt pressure from her to have Andy transferred, but I didn't feel peace about him leaving the PCU just yet. "Oh, Lord," I prayed, "Please give me wisdom. If it is not safe for Andy to leave the PCU, then please make a way for us to stay."

God often answers in ways we don't anticipate. The next day, Andy's lab test came back with a positive for C. diff (Clostridium difficile)—a contagious bacterial infection patients sometimes get when they've been on a large quantity of antibiotics. Consequently, Andy had to be in isolation for fourteen days until he tested negative for C. diff. During those first few days in isolation, Andy's blood pressure began to rise so high that the PCU couldn't treat it anymore. He had to be transferred back to the intensive care unit.

Back in the ICU, they took another angiogram, since it is not uncommon for patients to have another aneurysm once one has erupted. They found a third aneurysm in Andy's brain. My lack of peace about transferring Andy to the nursing home two weeks earlier suddenly made sense. They wouldn't have found the aneurysm in time, and Andy would have died. Once again, God had answered my prayers. Even though it wasn't in the way I'd expected, *it was God at work.*

This news of a third aneurysm hit me hard. The tests showed this aneurysm with a threat of rupturing was on a main vessel that controlled the right leg. The risk of Andy having a stroke during the next surgery was very high.

I was sitting in the ICU waiting room and asking God to not take Andy away from me, when I felt Him say, *I won't. There is still more work for you and Andy to do.*

"Is that You, God?" I asked. "Are You talking to me?"

Yes, He said. Then I looked up through the window, and I saw a little patch of blue sky shining through the gray clouds. I began to tear up. You see, I grew up in Hawaii, so seeing blue skies reminds me of home. When Andy and I moved to Portland, Oregon, the winters were very dreary, so I asked God to let me see patches of blue sky throughout that winter. He did, reminding me of His love every time. So when God gave me that patch of blue sky in the ICU waiting room, it was as if He'd given me a hug and confirmed His presence guiding us through this trial.

As Andy went into his third surgery, we asked everyone we knew to pray that it would be successful with no stroke or complications. Later in the night, Andy opened both his eyes. The saints prayed; God answered.

We thought that was the last one. But a week later, doctors found another aneurysm in his brain, on the part that controls the left side of his face and hands.

Dear Lord, I prayed, *let this be the last one.*

Our surgeon operated on Andy to clip the aneurysm in the right side of his brain. There was also some blood behind the aneurysm, which the surgeon took care of. Did the aneurysm start to bleed? Yes. Did God hold that aneurysm from rupturing? Yes.

That was God.

After two long months of living in the hospital, we were finally able to go to a skilled nursing facility. We were told that 60 percent of brain aneurysms result in death, but by the time we left the hospital, Andy had miraculously survived four brain aneurysms, with two of them rupturing before he could have surgery.

Although I'd always believed in prayer, it is cemented in me now. My heavenly Father indeed heard the pleas of His children— and answered. He still performs miracles—and there were just too many to count!

When Andy first fell down in the kitchen, I didn't even think to call 911. Later we were told that because we brought Andy in so quickly, his chances of survival had dramatically increased.

That was God.

I learned later that the doctors did not expect Andy to even wake up from the coma. His neurosurgeon said he beat 99.9 percent odds of death.

That was God.

I was very comfortable in my role as doctor's wife, and I had been just gliding through life. But like a rose bush that needed to be pruned, I needed to allow God to cut off my attitudes of pride and self-sufficiency. God gave me a renewed purpose, in His overflowing grace, to become a conduit of His grace and love. He showed me kindness so I could learn to extend kindness. I began wanting to do more than I ever did before—more giving, more grace, and more love.

That was God.

Two-and-a-half years after the first brain aneurysm, Andy started walking with a cane. His speech became clear, and his short-term and long-term memory started to return. He began feeding himself and showering with supervision. He started playing with a computer keyboard. We began working with a vision therapist to regain his right eye's visual field. Recently, Andy effortlessly walked his daughter, Anna, down the aisle on her wedding day. Andy works hard at all his therapies, but it is our God, our Lord Jesus Christ, who does the healing.

> *"Those who hope in the LORD will renew their strength. They will soar on wings like eagles; they will run and not grow weary, they will walk and not be faint." (Isaiah 40:31)*

I share this story with special thanks to our doctors: Dr. Vora, Dr. Riley, Dr. Faheeh, Dr. Beam, Dr. Degen, and Dr. Tilson; our nurses: Rebecca, Erika, Peggy, Bruce, Adrian, Sarah, Sheritia, Evelyn, Eric, Tsering, and Shan; our therapists: Michelle, Jeff, Lisa, Julie, Blaise, Hope, Vlad, Melissa, Andrew, Jamie, and Susan; our caregivers: John and Sakinah; our dear friends: Jon and Susan Guenther, David and Dawn Golobay, Rick and Barb Martin, Melvin and Lori Yamase, Lisa Kyukkyuk, and Linda Chelsky.

16

Breaking the Cycle

Mary Guess

I was born and raised in the small town of Brazil, Indiana. My father was in and out of prison for most of my childhood, since he was the town thief. My mother, brother, sisters, and I were living on welfare and dealing with all the stigma attached to our situation.

My mother was an angry, violent, and confused woman. It wasn't until later that I found out both she and my dad were victims of their parents' abuse. My mother told me that she loved me, but her actions didn't show love. If my siblings did something wrong, she blamed me. I was the eldest, after all. She beat me on a regular basis. I even got a lashing if I didn't move fast enough for her. I always wondered, *Do other mothers treat their children this way?* I often stayed away from home.

My mother would have me beg the neighbors or go to nearby family members for food or money. I didn't like begging, so at ten years old—when most little girls should be playing with dolls— I started mowing yards, raking leaves, babysitting, and working two paper routes to buy necessities for my family. I grew up fast. There were still countless times, when we would be painfully hungry, when a bag of groceries would miraculously appear on our doorstep. Even at ten, I felt God had His hand on my life.

77

When I was a freshman in high school, my grandfather's step-son, a senior named Sean, asked me to the prom. I wasn't sure why he asked me. Only the popular freshman girls got asked to go. No one had ever asked me on a date; it was a small town, my dad was in prison, and I was a welfare kid. So this was a big deal. And, strangely, my mom let me go. Sean's sister, Kelly, took me to a beauty salon where the stylist put my long brown hair into an updo and dressed me up in a beautiful sky-blue formal gown. I felt like a princess.

But things took a dark turn. Looking back, I am grateful we had made it a double date with Kelly and her boyfriend, because on the way home, Sean tried to rape me in the backseat of the car with Kelly and her boyfriend right there in the front. If Kelly hadn't stopped him by God's mercy, I would have been raped that night. I was scared to death. When I got home, I went right to bed and cried.

Traditionally, the day after prom, everyone went on a picnic. Sean showed up at my door to take me, but I refused to get out of bed. Even after I told my mom what had happened the night before, she insisted I go. She was concerned about Sean's feelings being hurt—that he would be embarrassed if I didn't go with him. But I determined not to move from my bed. As I lay there, my mom began to beat me. She pulled my hair, trying to yank me from the bed. Somehow, she couldn't move me. All the while, Sean was waiting outside.

So much for loving me, Mom! I thought. Yet the beating didn't hurt as much as her calling me stupid, telling me that no one would ever love me, and not protecting me from a potentially ter-rible situation. I'd had it. I was so hurt and angry that I promised myself I would leave home as soon as I could manage on my own, and that I would never get married and never have children.

One day, when I was spending time in prayer with the Lord, I asked Him, "Where were you when Sean was outside and my mom was beating me?"

Mary, I was right there with you, I felt Him say. *I was holding you on the bed—that's why your mom couldn't move you. Your mother chose to be angry and violent because that is what she knew, but I chose to protect you from things far worse than her anger.*

And then I felt Him say to me, *Trust Me, Mary, and follow Me. I will take you on a journey of change, choices, and victory.*

Two years later, as I was nearing my sixteenth birthday, my dad had served his time in prison and come home. He'd found a job and started working. One day he came home from work and told me that a "nice young man" was coming over to take me on a date Friday night, and that I should be ready to go at six o'clock. I made a point to refuse, but he wouldn't hear of it. Little did I know, God was working a miracle.

Before this time I'd been praying for God to send someone to love me. At lunchtime at school, two friends and I would sit in the balcony, sometimes pointing out boys we would date. One day I pointed to a boy and said, "If I was really desperate, I would go out with that guy."

I thought I was so funny. Well, the laugh was on me. It was that boy who showed up at my doorstep on Friday night. His name was Mike, and we soon began dating. While we were dating, my dad messed up again and was sent back to prison. I was sure that Mike wouldn't want to take me out anymore, and that his family wouldn't approve of me. After I told Mike about my dad, his response was, "I am in love with you, Mary, not your family." Does God answer prayer? Absolutely!

And so began my journey of redemption. Despite my promise to myself that I would never marry, Mike and I married two years later. And despite my promise that I would never have children—and the doctors telling us that we would probably never be able to—we have four beautiful children: David, Mark, Michelle, and Bethany. My relationship with the Lord continued to deepen, and He has helped me raise my wonderful children. Of course now I know the source of love is Jesus.

I continued to have a cordial relationship with my mom. She called on me many times for help, and I knew the Lord wanted me to be respectful to her and to care for her. But there was still a lot of hurt between us, and it wasn't until her father's funeral that I began to truly understand why.

At the funeral, my mom confessed to me that my grandfather had sexually molested her from the time she was three years old until she married my dad at the age of eighteen. I wanted to vomit. My heart broke for her and what she'd been through because of him. It explained her anger.

But then my mind went to a different place. She'd left my sister and me in his care many times. *How could she have done that?* I screamed inside. Yet I couldn't remember a time when he had ever harmed me. If he had, the Lord erased it from my memory. Still, this was very difficult for me to forgive. I wanted my mom to tell me she was sorry for how she'd treated me during my childhood. Instead, she looked at me and said that she'd done the best she could to raise me.

Ouch. That was hurtful. My heart was broken. Although my mother never apologized for her abuse, I learned that whether she asked for my forgiveness or not, forgiving her gave my heart permission to heal. I learned that although forgiving her didn't make her actions right, it allowed me to be free of bearing the burden of them in my life. The Lord helped me forgive my mother, and in the process, He took away the hurt I felt over my childhood so I could move on in my journey.

I realized that I had suffered from abuse because my parents had suffered from abuse, and they suffered from abuse because *their* parents suffered from abuse. It was a cycle that needed to stop with my family and me. I pledged to be the opposite of my mom, both as a wife and as a mother to my children. I was very involved in my children's lives, cherishing every moment with them and loving them deeply. Each one grew up thinking he or she was my favorite.

One day while I was driving, my daughter Bethany, a senior in high school at the time, sent me a text message. I pulled over to see that she had simply written "I love you, Mom."

Bethany had said she loved me a thousand times, but in that moment I felt God say to me, *Mary, the cycle has been broken!* I knew exactly what He meant. I wept tears of joy, and I praised the One who can heal all wounds.

Jesus didn't promise us a painless life, but with God's help, you and I can choose to not pass on the generational abuses of those before us. With His redeeming love and power, we can have a journey of change, choices, and victory.

> *Forget the former things; do not dwell on the past. See, I am doing a new thing! Now it springs up; do you not perceive it? I am making a way in the wilderness and streams in the wasteland. (Isaiah 43: 18-19)*

Mary Guess is blessed to be a wife and mother of four adult children plus their spouses and a grandma to ten. She is a friend and mentor to many. The generational curse has been lifted and has been replaced by God's love and respect for family and friends.

17

Born Without Fingers

Dawn Riverman

Born without fingers on his left hand, my son Dawson had to make a great effort to carry out the simplest of tasks, such as tying his shoes and holding a ball. At five years old, he came to me in my room and said, "Mom, I want a hand like everyone else. Why won't my hand grow?" What do you tell a five-year-old? I sat on the floor and cried with him.

We sought out many doctors and specialists but discovered no real answers. We even considered a high-tech prosthetic hand for him, but learned they are complicated medical devices powered by batteries and electronic motors. They can cost thousands of dollars, which we couldn't afford. Besides, some children who have them grow out of them too quickly to make the investment practical. So most children do without, fighting to do with one hand what most of us do with two.

Though Dawson was healthy in every other way, other children teased and stared at him. He'd hide his hand behind his back during interactions with anyone besides family.

I prayed earnestly that God would allow Dawson to have two hands one day.

For seven years I researched solutions. Then one day I had a conversation with one of Dawson's teachers that gave me hope.

She put me in touch with a husband-and-wife team who owned a new type of invention—a three-dimensional printer—that could possibly help my son. This technology uses a high-power laser to fuse small particles of plastic, metal, ceramic, or glass powders into a mass that has the desired three-dimensional shape.

Soon after I contacted them, my family traveled to visit them in hopes of finally seeing our dream of a functional left hand come true. Jen and Ivan opened their home to us and showed us how to build a prosthetic hand for Dawson—a three-dimensional, printed hand. The results were amazing! It took about ten hours to print, and another two to three hours to assemble, but the final result was we had a cobalt blue and black hand for Dawson.

It wasn't much harder than putting together a complex Lego kit. The hand is made from a durable type of thermoplastic, weighs less than a pound, and fits him perfectly.

Upon leaving Jen and Ivan's home, we asked what we owed them for this incredible gift of a new hand for Dawson. My tears overflowed at their response: "You owe us nothing." Instead, they asked us to donate to the organization they volunteer with that provides 3-D hands for children all over the world. (Globally, one in a thousand babies are born without a full set of fingers.)

Now at thirteen, Dawson can ride a bike and hold a baseball bat. He's even playing goalkeeper on his soccer team. He's realizing he can now do things with two hands and not have to try to figure out every movement.

Our family is working with our children's school to get a 3-D printer so students can make 3-D hands to give to children around the world on our annual mission trips.

I believe God inspired the inventors of 3-D printing. Dawson is only one of potentially millions of people whose lives will be drastically improved by these prosthetics. Not only did God answer our prayer for providing two complete hands for Dawson, but He has also given Dawson an opportunity to make a big impact by making prosthetics for children in other countries.

Come and hear, all you who fear God; let me tell you what he has done for me. I cried out to him with my mouth; his praise was on my tongue…God has surely listened and has heard my prayer. (Psalm 66:16-17,19)

Dawn Riverman and her family are thankful for e-NABLE, a volunteer organization aiming to match children like Dawson with volunteers able to make prosthetics on 3-D printers. www .enablingthefuture.org

18

Lost Coin

LAUREN FREY

I like to take the time to pick up lost pennies. Of course a quarter, dime, or nickel is more exciting to find. But pennies? The useless copper coins? The ones that get kicked around until they stick to the ground on some chewed-up piece of gum? Yes. I've found around a hundred of them so far. I keep them in a jar. I'm a dollar richer, now, thank you very much.

One day, I found more than a penny. Actually, it found me. It wasn't on a sidewalk, but in a church while I was on a mission trip in my home state of Oregon. Our team of fifteen from my California-based ministry school only had one mission: to flood the streets with "the evidence of things unseen"—with the supernatural yet tangible love of the Father.

Tuesday morning, the fourth day our trip, I woke up and read Matthew 7:7: "Ask and it will be given to you; seek and you will find; knock and the door will be opened to you." I felt God tell me that He was serious about that. He meant to give my team and me things we asked for by grace, in faith, and in His Name. He wanted the things of His kingdom to be received, found, and opened.

Lord, what does that look like? I prayed. *Teach me today.*

Later that day, the team was having a meeting in our host church's office. Before the meeting began, a team member, Jared, showed me a Bible verse that had struck him that morning. He was reading it from one translation, and I got curious about how the verse read in another. I walked over to the church's shelf of donated Bibles. A baby-pink Bible, spine all worn, caught my eye. When I sat back down on the couch and flipped it open, a crisp and perfectly folded hundred-dollar bill fell from the pages. Who knows where it came from?

"Jared, look! This just fell out of this Bible."

"What?" he said, smiling. "Are you serious?"

I held it up to the light. "It's real!"

I took it to the pastor. "Um, Pastor Jim, this just fell from a spare Bible." I tried to give it to him.

"No, no," he said with a grin, pushing it back into my hand. "Keep it. I believe God has something for you to do with it."

As the meeting began, I tucked it away in my red wallet. *Okay, God. That was cool. Will you show me what You want to do with this?*

Two days later, on a rainy afternoon in downtown Portland, we had a two-hour time slot to go out on the streets and pray for anyone the Lord led us to. I grabbed my purse, an umbrella, and a simple drawing of the word "freedom" with flying birds in the middle that I'd drawn the night before. Then along with two team members, Lindy and Michael, I started walking toward the waterfront.

"Lord, lead us," we prayed out loud. "Show us who You want us to minister to today."

We walked two blocks when a woman caught our eye. And then we caught hers.

"Excuse me!" she cried to us. "Do you know where Pioneer Square is?"

"Are you new around here?" we asked.

"Yes," she said.

Michael, who was familiar with the city, gave her directions to the square. But since it seemed God had highlighted her to us or us to her—however that had worked—we knew we were supposed to keep talking with her.

"What's your name?"

"Leah," she replied.

"What brought you to Portland?"

Leah told us she'd just been released after four years in prison. She also told us she'd become a Christian and was basically homeless, in need of money, in need of a job, looking for a fresh start, and seeking a church to fellowship in.

Lindy asked Leah if we could pray for her.

She said yes.

As we started praying for her right there in the hustle-bustle of the streets, she started tearing up. The Holy Spirit's presence became so strong as we felt Him guiding our prayers and giving us specific words of encouragement for Leah. After a few minutes of praying, the Holy Spirit reminded me of the money in my wallet.

"Leah," I said, "I have something to give you."

I first gave her my umbrella, and then the picture that said "freedom," and finally the hundred-dollar bill. When she received it, she started crying even more. It looked like God had given her a hug that nearly knocked her over.

"No way!" she finally said. "You won't believe this." Leah told us that earlier on that very morning, an old friend from her past life had contacted her, asking her to help with a drug deal. It would have been a $200 deal, and she would have been paid half.

"But I refused to do it," she told us. "I told God, 'No, I am not going to do this. I believe You will provide for me.'"

We were speechless. "Leah, God *loves* you!" we said.

"I know," she said, through tears, as if realizing it afresh.

I'll never forget the beautiful smile beaming from her face as she recognized that her heavenly Father heard her prayers, knew her heart, honored her faith and obedience, and had miraculously provided for her—all in one day. We prayed with her again and gave her some names of ministries and churches to plug into in the Portland area, including the church that was hosting us.

I know what it's like to search for pennies. But I admit, they are pretty worthless. This hunt doesn't do anything for me—except remind me of the joy that God provides.

If I find just a little joy in finding pennies, imagine the joy God feels when He finds—or rather *reclaims*—something of true value: a child of His. Jesus told three parables of lost things being found: one of a hundred sheep, one of ten coins, and one of two sons (Luke 15). Jesus enjoys finding things too—lost things.

While I was absolutely blown away to witness God give Leah the unmerited grace of provision that day, I also felt unmerited grace in my life to partner with Him in the process. I didn't deserve to be the one to give Leah that money. I will never be worthy of giving what is God's. Even *that* is by grace. But God answered my prayer to teach me more about what it looks like to live out of His kingdom—a kingdom with endless storehouses of things to be readily received, found, and opened.

Most of all, He instilled in me a fresh hunger that day to live with more awareness of Him, the pursuing Father of all, who is ever seeking and saving what is lost.

There is joy in the presence of God's angels when even one sinner repents. (Luke 15:10 NLT)

Lauren Frey is currently studying English literature and writing at a university in California.

19

A Child's Prayer

Ginny Mooney

I was ten years old. We'd just buried my Uncle Al a week earlier. It had been my first funeral. We children sat off to the side in a section partially cordoned off with a curtain so that we could hear the service but not see the body—my uncle's body.

Just a few days before, Uncle Al had been perfectly fine, at least on the outside. He'd gone into the hospital for open-heart surgery, but he never came out. My Aunt Evie, whose birthday I share, was inconsolable. They'd met and married when she was fifty. It was her first marriage, and they'd had only five years together. She wailed over and over again, "How could this happen?" She stood in the parking lot of the funeral home sobbing, refusing to go in. My father tried to console her, and in that moment, something happened—Aunt Evie said God touched her and a wave of complete peace descended on her. After that, it seemed everything would be okay.

One week after the funeral, I came home from school to find my mother worried and upset. She explained my dad had gone in for his yearly checkup and they found something wrong with his heart—a blockage.

A blockage? thought my ten-year-old self. Panic raced through me. "What does that mean?" I asked.

My mom gently explained that a blockage means blood can't flow to and from the heart freely. The blockage was fairly large, the doctors thought, and they might have to operate. But before they did that, they would do one more test to measure the exact size and to confirm its location. This procedure was called a catheterization.

That word was big and scary, but it wasn't as scary to me as the word *operate.* I knew an operation meant surgery. Wasn't it heart surgery that Uncle Al had just undergone and not survived? I was shocked. *My father could die. Die! How would I ever survive that?* My dad was more than just my father; he was my hero. Every day after school, my sister, brother, and I watched for him to come home from work. We ran to the door to meet him and climb on him as if he were a human jungle gym. My dad was kind and gentle. He made us laugh. He loved people, and they loved him. He rarely passed my mom or us children in the house without giving us a kiss on the cheek or a little squeeze. Even when my dad worked late, he would come home and check my homework for the next day. I didn't just love Dad; I adored him. Now he might go away, just like Uncle Al had.

As I thought things over in my ten-year-old heart, I knew there was only one Person who could save my father. I went quietly to my room and got down on my knees by my bed, as I'd seen my father do every night for as long as I could remember. I clasped my hands, looked up, and spoke to God:

> Lord, please, please, please don't take my father away. Please! I love him so much, and we all need him. Mom needs him, I need him, and Jennifer and John need him. Please, Lord, heal him if You can. But please don't take him away.

I didn't stop praying. I pleaded with God over and over again, every day, up to the day of his test. Sometimes as I prayed I thought about the way God had answered my aunt Evie's prayers for help by reaching down and comforting her so she could go on after Uncle Al's death. His answer to Aunt Evie was a good answer, but it wasn't the kind of answer I wanted from God. Not at all!

The day came for my dad's test. As we left for school, Dad and Mom assured us all that everything would be okay. I nodded and smiled, not wanting them to see my fear. They had enough to worry about. I went to school that day and kept praying through classes, lunch, and recess. I had heard that God always answered prayers, but what kind of answer would it be?

I raced into the house after school. My mom came to greet me, smiling. *Maybe the blockage wasn't as big as they thought. Maybe they wouldn't have to do surgery at all. Or maybe it could wait a while.*

"You'll never believe what happened, Ginny," my mom said as we sat on the couch together. "The doctors went in with the catheter, and they couldn't find the blockage. They couldn't find *any* blockage! It was completely gone. They didn't know what to think. They were completely amazed." And then she added with a smile, "Daddy's heart is just fine."

The doctors might not have known what to think, but I did! I hugged my mom tight and then ran to my room and got back down on my knees. I looked up with a giant smile on my face even as I tasted the salt of tears.

"Thank You, God! Thank You," I said over and over again. "Thank You for giving me my dad back!"

Since that day more than thirty-five years ago, there have been many times God has answered my prayers in ways other than what I wanted. Sometimes He's said, "No," or "Not now." Pastors tell us He is teaching us patience or trust when He does that. I'm sure they are right. But on that one glorious day long ago, God said a big "Yes!" to a little girl's anxious prayers. He knew I needed my daddy. And that is an act of my other Father's love I will never forget.

> [Jesus said,] "If you sinful people know how to give good gifts to your children, how much more will your heavenly Father give good gifts to those who ask Him." (Matthew 7:11 NLT)

Ginny Mooney is a freelance writer and Emmy Award-winning television producer. She lives in Florida with her two children, Azalea and Asher.

20

Unexpected, Beautiful Joy

LILY CROWDER

I grew up in a Christian home, though it was very broken and dysfunctional. I was raised with the knowledge of Christ, but I became the typical Christian good girl gone bad. After a series of sad events and foolish choices, I turned away from my faith and was basically plain ol' naughty. The unwise choices I kept making and the harmful people I kept migrating toward left me in a state of depression and emptiness. I knew what was right and godly, but I refused to live that way. I hated myself for it. My struggle with identity and feelings of unworthiness made me hungry for healthy affirmation and affection. I was your classic young woman "looking for love in all the wrong places." It wasn't too long before I ended up pregnant at the age of eighteen.

I had to humbly face my old Christian community and small-town friends, move in with my mom, and live on welfare. It was such a lonely, humiliating time in my life. Being knocked-up and abandoned by someone who had claimed to care for me was overwhelmingly heartbreaking, to say the least.

For the duration of my pregnancy, I focused on trying to get my life back together. I had a desperate hunger to make up for all the wrong I'd done. I felt so undeserving of anything good. I thought I was going to be punished for all my sins and that God was going to give me a horribly challenging baby. I felt so alone, undeserving, unworthy, unfit, worthless, and scared. I asked God to turn the mess I had made into something beautiful.

When my labor finally came on, I had no idea what was about to happen. I could only anticipate an outcome from a place of fear, rejection, and uncertainty. But despite my fragile state, I could feel the love and gentleness of Jesus. That day changed my life forever.

I gave birth to a beautiful and healthy baby girl. She was amazing—so perfect, such a tiny wonder. In those first few moments with her, I couldn't help but thank and praise the Lord for her life. My love for her came from deep within and was overwhelming and unexpected. I never knew that love this deep for another person existed. I named her Maile (pronounced *My-lee*, which is Hawaiian for "beautiful") Joy.

Knowing I didn't deserve such a gift, I asked God, "What about my punishment? I did everything wrong, and yet here I am holding this beautiful, perfect baby girl—a perfect gift." Every day she got cuter. She had two huge dimples when she smiled and glorious, perfect baby rolls. She was so happy. To this day, I still call her "Smiley Maile."

As a new mom, I felt God's grace and presence in the ways He provided a natural, new love and inspiration in me for Maile. When all my friends were out on the town and I was home alone with my baby, I knew God had a plan and that Maile was one of the best parts of it. I really enjoyed being a mom—even a single mom. Maile and I did everything together. God also provided me a job as a nanny so I was able to take my baby girl with me to work. Because of her wonderful demeanor, I was even able to take her to my college classes.

At times, I would still think of her future and the lack of a father. I would feel guilty for my inability to provide everything I thought she needed. Those feelings were often paralyzing. Yet I would talk to God about it. I asked Him to provide what we needed most in His way and timing.

The day after I turned twenty-two, I met a tall, dark, hand-some, and witty man named John. I could barely stand when I first spoke to him, and nor could he. Something in me knew that he was "the one." Yet I was afraid. Later on I even tried to hide from him in the basement of the church where we met. It was so obvious to everyone around us that there was more than chemistry between us. It was love. For the first time in my life I felt real, supernatural love.

Along with falling in love with me, John also fell in love with my little blue-eyed girl. While we were engaged, and while John was away on a work trip, he wrote me a letter confessing what was taking place in his heart for my little girl. The idea of being her father was effortless and natural, as if it had always been part of the plan.

John adopted Maile shortly after we were married. She was three at the time, and has grown to know and trust him as if he's always been with us from the very first day. Maile became, and is still to this day, daddy's girl. The bond and connection they share is amazing to see. Since our marriage, God has blessed John and me with three more delightful children.

Before I met John, I remember a time when my daughter was about two. I was alone in my little home, and I opened my Bible for the first time in a long while. I found myself reading Luke 7:47: "I tell you, her many sins have been forgiven—as her great love has shown. But whoever has been forgiven little loves little." I am so thankful that because I have been forgiven much, God has enabled me to not only love again but to love much.

I still remember the feeling of being an outsider. When I see a young girl or single mom who is struggling, I'm able to encourage her by sharing my story. I truly wouldn't trade this transformation and what God has done for anything, even with all the awkward and hard moments involved. God's love unexpectedly burst into my life and made things new.

We love because [God] first loved us. (1 John 4:19)

Lily Crowder, *Grace for the Contemplative Parent* (Marylhurst, OR: Sons of Thunder Ministries & Publications, 2013), pp. 11-15. Edited and used by permission.

Lily Crowder is a devoted wife and mother and cofounder of Sons of Thunder Ministries and Publications.

21

Impostors, Yet True

BILL MacLEOD

A few years before the disintegration of the Iron Curtain and communism across Western Europe, I was an unmarried twentysomething who had just finished working with Luis Palau on a citywide evangelistic campaign in northeast Scotland. I had started a hitchhiking trip across Europe. Bible smuggling on the side was not exactly in my plan; but as I was hitchhiking, I met a seasoned worker of Christ who was adept in this undertaking.

The man invited me to come with him to take Hungarian Bibles into Hungary's capital city, Budapest. Despite the news that in the past few months other mission groups had been imprisoned for what we were about to do, we carefully loaded boxes of Bibles into his car's secret compartments and started toward the Austrian–Hungarian border.

As we approached the city of Sopron where the crossing would take place, I opened my Bible. The Lord took me to verses I'd never noticed before—2 Corinthians 6:4-8, where the apostle Paul gave a defense of his sacrifice in ministry, saying they were considered "impostors, and yet are true" (verse 8 ESV). I realized that to surreptitiously hide these Bibles and risk carrying them across this border would require me to be an impostor. And yet in this, I was being true to the call on my life: to spread the gospel of Jesus Christ.

Just before the border, we pulled the car over to pray for our safety and deliverance. Then we drove up to the tall, barbed-wire fences where uniformed, armed guards in turrets looked down on us. After other guards searched the inside of the car, they carefully examined the outside again and then let us pass.

Once we were on our way, my friend lifted his finger to his lips as if to stop me from saying anything. Sure enough, just a little further ahead, we were halted again at another entry point. Between the two entry points, listening devices were used to pick up conversations of unassuming travelers who were unfamiliar with the lengths at which the authorities were taking to determine their visitors' true intentions.

When we arrived in Budapest, we found the house church of Hungarian believers who worshipped in secret. They would receive the Bibles. I met a man about my age who had spent his entire four years of military duty in jail simply because he was an unashamed follower of Jesus. In the faces of these vibrant believers, I saw something that I lacked. Even with my access to Scripture and freedom to worship and fellowship, I felt naked. *They* were the ones magnificently clothed. They were impostors, and yet true.

The time came for us to make the exchange of our precious cargo. We drove around in our car, and they followed us in theirs, looking for a concealed location in the dark. Finally, we chose a spot on the side of the road, about a hundred yards away from a brightly lit factory. Everyone scurried with their heads down between the two cars to transfer the Bibles as quickly as possible. Suddenly, someone looked up and saw a guard from the factory approaching.

Our transaction came to a chaotic halt. Doors and trunks slammed, and we screeched down the road before the guard could reach us. My heart was pounding, and I quickly learned that missionaries have to become good at improvising. We fervently prayed as we drove around looking for another site to finish the exchange. Finally, we found a secluded, pitch-dark vacant lot on the side of a road further up into the hills. After looking it over, we made our move. The Bibles were safely and swiftly shuffled without incident. After a quick thank you and farewell to our friends, we drove our separate ways into the night. We were impostors, and yet true.

We drove back to the border with a greater sense of relief and peace than we'd had when we'd entered. But as the guard motioned for us to step out of the car so it could be examined, I glanced at the backseat. To my horror, I noticed I had left the Celtic Bible I had brought with me from Scotland in plain sight. The guard immediately picked it up and started looking through it.

The "mission accomplished" feeling evaporated in an instant, and the words in 2 Corinthians 6:8, which had been bringing me such conviction and hope, suddenly felt powerless—as did I. Inside, I cried out to the Lord. Lifting my head and eyes toward the distant Hungarian hills of Sopron, I immediately remembered the distinctly comforting words of Psalm 121:

> I lift up my eyes to the hills. From where does my help come? My help comes from the LORD, who made heaven and earth...The LORD will keep you from all evil; he will keep your life. The LORD will keep your going out and your coming in from this time forth and forevermore. (vv. 1-2, 7-8 ESV)

The guard couldn't read the language the Bible was written in, so he turned to me for an explanation. I remember mumbling something about it being "just a book." *Just a book, indeed!* For a moment he hesitated, and then he threw it back onto the seat. He hastily motioned for us to leave.

No one had to sign for me to be quiet this time as we sped toward Vienna. We drove in silence for a few miles, taking in the care, protection, and wonder of God. It was a short journey, yet sufficient for the journey of a lifetime. God delivered us. We were impostors, and yet true.

We are treated as impostors, and yet are true. (2 Corinthians 6:8 ESV)

Bill MacLeod has been a mission mobilizer for more than thirty years, dedicated to citywide people movements while serving in an evangelistic organization, in a national men's movement, and as a local church missions pastor. He currently serves as the founder and executive director of Mission ConneXion, a church-missions mobilizing effort.

22

Yahweh Rophe

Ferol Chew

It was a beautiful spring day when I waved my fifteen-year-old son, Aaron, a loving goodbye as he got on his moped to visit a friend. Little did I know that within the next ten minutes our world would be shaken.

As Aaron approached a frequently visited public garden, a van stopped in front of him, attempting to turn into the garden's entrance. Aaron didn't see it stop. He drove headlong into the back of the van, flying over the moped's handlebars, breaking both legs as he landed, and knocking himself unconscious. He had severe head trauma. Within minutes, he was rushed to the hospital where he went directly into surgery.

It wasn't until three hours later, as I was fixing dinner, that I received the news of the accident. The phone rang. It was one of Aaron's friends who had heard he'd crashed on the moped. I dropped everything as fear crushed my heart. I told my husband, Larry, and we started calling emergency rooms in the area. Thankfully, the second place that picked up the phone informed us that they indeed had an accident victim who fit Aaron's description and that he was in surgery.

When Larry and I arrived at the hospital's intensive care unit, a neurosurgeon informed us that only 50 percent of patients with

Aaron's types of injuries live. There were no gentle words and no compassion. Just brutal facts—and the worst kind a parent can possibly hear. He also told us that if Aaron survived, he would never be the same mentally.

Aaron was given multiple blood transfusions. A probe was inserted into his skull to relieve pressure and to watch for signs that would tell doctors he needed more surgery. Both legs were set, and the very bad compound fracture of the left thigh was put in traction. He had bruised kidneys. For five days, he remained unconscious in the ICU due to his severe head injuries.

Now, prayer is something we don't need to do on our own. During this time our pastors, church family, friends, Aaron's sister, and Aaron's grandparents never left our side. These prayer warriors didn't let us give up. Together we asked *Yahweh-Rophe*, the Lord who Heals, to spare and heal Aaron's broken body, while keeping our focus on God's power to do so.

Life in the hospital was filled with fragile moments. We didn't know how many days we would be there and what kind of news would end each day. One day I retreated by myself into a dark room. With a breaking, fearful, and defeated heart, I cried out to God and gave my precious child up to Him. Aaron had always been strong in his faith and loved God, but I prayed that if it were Aaron's time to go, that God would receive him. It was the hardest thing I had ever done, for although I had prayed and given him to God before, in this moment I gave his *life* over to God. I let go of him and rededicated him to God. I put the whole situation in God's hands.

Aaron remained in ICU for eleven days, at the end of which his body began to heal. After thirty days, he was ready to come home. After months of rehab and physical therapy, Aaron proved the doctors wrong. During the last doctor's visit, the doctor confessed: "It wasn't medicine that healed your son."

Not only did Aaron live but his mind and body were made completely normal. The accident in no way affected the way he walks or lives now—with the exception of some metal in one leg, which is only noticeable when he walks through metal detectors at airport security. He's a carpenter and very active young man.

God heard our prayers when we cried out. He answered us as we depended on His mercy and power. It was up to us to trust God's sovereign ways of love. My job was, and is, to allow His Word to confront my fears and hold me close through the deepest of valleys as He lives in me and leads me on.

Now faith is the substance of things hoped for, the evidence of things not seen. (Hebrews 11:1 NKJV)

Ferol Chew is a mentor and fourteen-year Bible study leader in her church. She and her husband, Larry, are involved with several church activities, an outreach, and a shepherd group ministry.

23

The Bear

BILL SUNDSTROM

I was a young believer on spring break my freshman year in college. My friends Dan and Buck invited me to go on a backpacking trip in the Porcupine Mountains of Northern Michigan. As three carefree young guys, we roamed and hiked around, sometimes talking to fellow travelers about the Lord. We didn't even have a tent—just a piece of plastic we rigged up as a lean-to for sleeping. Toward the end of our seven-day trip, we ran clean out of food.

"No problem," we said. "We'll just do a little fishing."

We were far from any regular campgrounds, so we pitched our lean-to in a random spot near Lake Superior. Tossing our lines in a little stream that ran by our camp, we tried our luck. All we could catch were suckers—bony little fish generally considered inedible. But we were starving, so we cleaned and ate them anyway. After dinner, we carelessly tossed the bones into the woods near our campsite.

That night as we were sitting around the campfire, we heard something big crashing around nearby.

"Squirrels?" I said hopefully.

"No way," Buck replied. "Too big."

In that moment, we all remembered the ranger's warning before we took off: "Watch out for bears."

I thought of how exposed we were, with not even a real tent to hide in. Dan suggested we pray. In my young faith, I wasn't sure God could handle this, but it still sounded good to me. Dan prayed and asked the Lord to send the bear somewhere else, since we were His servants and had been trying to trust Him and make Him known on this trip.

Then we went to sleep under our lean-to tent and passed the night in peace. The next morning, we found fresh bear droppings about a hundred yards down the trail. We soon learned that two couples a few hundred yards on the other side of us had cowered in their tents and watched a bear rip open their packs looking for food. Not only had he taken their food, but he'd eaten forty hits of speed as well.

And there we were, right between the two points the bear had been. The drugged bear must have walked—or floated—amid the trees and right through our campsite to get from one point to the other. I was amazed that God really had answered our prayer.

Yet it seemed the Lord wanted to drive the point home. An hour or so later, Buck went down to the shoreline of Lake Superior to collect driftwood for a fire. As he was about to toss a log on the fire, Dan said: "Wait a minute! It looks like there are words on that piece of driftwood."

Dan grabbed the jagged section of the two-by-four board and cleaned the dirt off. As the words emerged, we gasped. There on that weather-beaten piece of driftwood somebody had carved the words: *God answers prayer.*

God is our refuge and strength, an ever-present help in trouble. (*Psalm 46:1*)

As a former writer and editor with *Worldwide Challenge* magazine, **Bill Sundstrom** has traveled the globe in pursuit of stories, visiting some seventy countries along the way. Whether telling about a villager in the Andes, a banker in London, or a bear in the woods, he gets to the heart of a story and brings distant places and people to life. Bill and his wife have three children and live in Pennsylvania.

24

The Fourth Child

Dinah Schild Nicholson

I was lying on the sun-soaked wood floor of my childhood home staring at a photo in a magazine. *Thirteen children*. It was a photograph of Harry and Bertha Holt, of Holt International Children's Services, and their large family. I was five years old and the youngest of five children. I knew what it was like to be part of a big family, yet what held my attention most was that eight of these children were Korean. They were adopted. At that moment, God planted a seed in my heart for adoption.

My first plan was to plead with my parents to adopt a little sister or brother. I was unrelenting, yet all my five-year-old charms were insufficient. Then the Holy Spirit whispered into my heart, *One day* you *will adopt your own child.*

I presumed He meant I would adopt if I were unable to give birth. Thirty-one years later, however, I was happily married to a supportive and loving husband, Steve, with whom I had three children during our first five years of marriage.

Steve and I were extremely busy with full-time careers in the financial services arena. In addition, we were in the throes of bringing our clients through the 1987 market crash. That year, to my astonishment, I heard God's voice whisper, "You shall have a fourth child." And I knew He meant it was time to adopt.

My exhausted husband suggested we wait five years. In that time, God didn't remove my passion to adopt. While volunteering for an adoption agency, we continued to pray and talk about it. We eventually named this dilemma "the fourth-child issue."

One day, I compared the reasons for buying a boat, which was my husband's dream, to adopting a fourth child. The pros and cons were almost identical, except that it would be hard to hug a boat and one can't waterski behind a child.

We entered into counseling, both of us hoping to convince my heart that adopting a fourth child would be unwise with our overpacked schedules. But after the counselors listened to us, they concluded we should adopt! God was a gentleman, and He waited for our free-will decision. And now, years later, we often laugh about the moment when my husband retorted, "You didn't tell me that you wanted to adopt a child before we were married."

"If I had told you all my dreams and passions," I quickly replied, "you would have been afraid to marry me!"

In faith, we started the adoption process. We involved the entire family in the decision, and we agreed to pursue adopting from a Russian orphanage. By the end of 1996, we had passed the home study screening, completed many forms, jumped through the usual hoops, and dealt with setbacks.

In January of the next year, the adoption agency showed us the medical report of a healthy three-year-old girl named Galina Valentinovna Merzlyakova. She was born on Christmas Eve 1993, which was a night I vividly remembered having a heartfelt talk with God about the "fourth child" calling.

After a slow, all-night train ride through the Ural Mountains, we arrived in Serov, Russia, on March 11, 1997. It was a cold and snowy morning. We stepped off the muggy train into the cool air. When we finally reached the front door of the orphanage, we felt like Lucy in C. S. Lewis' *The Lion, Witch, and Wardrobe*, walking through the back of the wardrobe and into a new season and territory.

Within an hour, our new daughter Galina Victoria Nicholson ("Tori") was in our arms. She was tiny for a three-year-old, at only twenty-three pounds and thirty inches tall. She was shy, of course, but excited. We instantly won her over by blowing soap bubbles.

We learned years later that Galina was born prematurely as the eleventh child of a very poor family. The Russian government had already removed three of the family's children to an orphanage, and the maternity ward wouldn't allow the birth mother to take Galina home. Our baby spent the first three months of her life in the hospital before being transferred to the orphanage in Serov.

Tori is now twenty years old. She is spunky, courageous, friendly, and trusting. Steve and I remind Tori that God always had a plan for her and that His hand is still on her. We are thankful that her heart is with God and that she has conversations with Him. Raising and loving her has been one of the greatest pleasures of our lives.

To quote Bertha Holt, the woman God used in my life when I was five years old: "All children are beautiful when they're loved."*

You received God's Spirit when he adopted you as his own children. Now we call him, "Abba, Father." (Romans 8:15 NLT)

*See at https://www.holtinternational.org/historybg.shtml.

Dinah Schild Nicholson is a retired certified financial planner, married to Steve, and mother to four Christ-loving adult children. She is currently being trained in neuro-behavior models used with Fetal Alcohol Spectrum disorders.

25

Beating Autism

BERNADETTE S.

Jacob, our eldest son, was only three years old when the words *Autism, Attention Deficit Disorder, Sensory Integration Disorder*, and *Asperger's Syndrome* became commonplace in our home. These diagnoses for Jacob helped explain why he didn't act like other children. He was so sensitive that even wind physically hurt his skin. Often the sound of a lawnmower at the end of our street would send him into a frenzy, and sudden laughter in our home would make him cry. At church, the only way to keep him happy was to *be* the Sunday school teacher.

I knew Jacob would never be "normal," but I hoped he would learn how to overcome the challenges he faced. I knew God doesn't make any mistakes, so He didn't make one when He made Jacob.

I prayed God would prove Himself faithful to Jacob, helping him with every difficult circumstance he faced and giving him God's peace in our loud and busy world. I prayed Jacob would be able to live a normal and productive life, learning how to channel his gifts for God's glory. I wanted Jacob to live certain that God made him with a plan and purpose.

Although my husband and I had planned for me to work in a teaching job while we raised our kids, doing so would require sending Jacob to daycare, something I knew he wasn't ready for. So earning money from home was the next best option. Although I went to school to become a teacher, art had always been my first love. Staying home with Jacob jumpstarted my art career. God blessed the endeavor, providing me not only with many jobs and projects, but also with the ability to be a stay-at-home mom.

When it was time for Jacob to go to school, many people counseled me that he would probably need to be in a special program or be homeschooled. But the local school worked with us. Jacob's first-grade teacher, knowing that he needed a sense of safety and structure, designed a storybook for him with large pictures of himself in the school with various teachers. Using this, she would tell Jacob to go to the page of the classroom they were currently in, such as his "library page," when they were in the library. This helped him with transitions. She also let me work with him and sit with him in the classroom until the other students arrived.

As his first-grade year progressed, my sitting with him eventually turned into standing by the door, and then waiting down the hall. Finally, on the last day of the school year, I only walked with him to the front door of the school. It was thrilling to see him overcoming his fears. He wasn't only surviving, but he was also thriving in school. I couldn't wait to share this exciting news with the women in my Moms in Prayer group. They'd all been praying along with me that Jacob would successfully make the necessary transition into public school. We all rejoiced in seeing how God was answering our prayers.

Making friends became his next great challenge. Other kids felt uncomfortable around him because he often shook his hands uncontrollably or cried over minor things. I tried to organize play-dates with other moms and kids so Jacob could find a friend. It was a struggle for him to feel like he could fit in. His physician told us he would learn to overcome autistic struggles, but his behavioral tendencies wouldn't change. Jacob would always struggle with loud noises, sudden changes, and staying on task.

Jacob learned to cope with his sensory issues through a sport he loved—running. I couldn't believe my eyes when the boy who cried because of the wind and the loud lawn mowers positioned himself to run following a piercing shot from a starting gun. Yes, he was still afraid of the noise, but his determination and faith were his lifelines. And unlike other competitive and team sports, this was something he could really do! It was exciting to see his confidence increase and, with it, his circle of friends. By his senior year of high school, we found it hard to find family time because he always had something to do with others.

During this final year of high school, we saw him overcome the social and behavioral obstacles of autism and flourish in school. Jacob had to work extra hard to keep his grades up. He took twice as long to finish assignments, and he would come home after school and sit in the same chair for hours to complete his homework. His diligence to attend to his studies despite his disabilities resulted in a grade point average of almost 3.9. After initial hurdles, his disability helped him make good friends; his love and kindness came from his high sensitivity to the people around him.

Jacob began to consider becoming a physical therapist. When we took him to look at colleges, the program he wanted to get into was very competitive, demanding, and required seven years of college education. Yet he was absolutely resolute in his decision. We were concerned about our ability to provide finances. Then we received a phone call telling us that our dear friend Myrna had passed away. Myrna and her husband, Dick, who had passed away a year earlier, never acted as if they had much money. But they had apparently saved diligently, wanting to be a blessing to our boys. They had left quite an inheritance for our two sons.

One month before Jacob's high school graduation, I found myself handing each son a check, reminding them that God was making a way for them to go to college. Their eyes widened as they looked down at $50,000, and more was coming.

Though God has not answered every prayer in my life, God's gifts are always good. He does hear our prayers. The little boy who would not separate from me and could not be around many people at once now has a big heart for people, for life, and for God. He knows that it was God alone who saw him through it all.

My entire family, including all those who have prayed with me for Jacob over the years, has learned so much from him about what it means to trust God. We can say wholeheartedly that God has a hope and a future for all who call on Him.

"I know the plans that I have for you," declares the LORD, "plans for welfare and not for calamity to give you a future and a hope." (Jeremiah 29:11 NASB)

Bernadette is a professional artist who creates numerous watercolor and acrylic paintings on commission, and teaches art classes to students ages five to seventy. Her miracle son Jacob is thriving in college.

26

Finding Rest

ADAM NEAL

It was 1962 when the doctor looked at me and said, "My prescription for you is this: Get rest and a change of pace."

I was a thirty-one-year-old sales manager for a company with high expectations and quotas to meet. Despite working day and night, I wasn't producing enough. My boss would tell me, "Thanks at least for the try." My anxiety and exhaustion grew and grew until it became more than I could handle.

I knew the doctor was right. I desperately needed rest, but how could I rest with a wife and two small children to support? Slowing down to take a breather didn't seem financially possible. So I worked harder, becoming more exhausted, full of fear, and eventually distrustful of everyone, including my wife. Finally, I became too weak to work. I was admitted to the hospital after having a complete nervous breakdown.

For six weeks I stayed in the hospital. During this time, I asked God for His healing touch. Those weeks became God's time to speak to my heart and give me assurance of His peace and love, which allowed my fears to eventually dissipate. I drenched myself in the Scriptures, especially in the book of Psalms. I committed myself anew to God, to getting well, and to learning to trust people again.

Meanwhile, my wife, Amy, started working to provide for our family's financial needs. The doctor warned her that I might never work again. She was devastated, but knew nevertheless that she was to trust and lean on the Lord for His peace, comfort, and support.

By the end of the six weeks, my health and outlook on life had been restored so much that the doctors released me early and I was allowed to stop taking medication. While the doctors may have expected me to relapse, I felt in my heart that God really had healed me.

A week after I was discharged, Amy and I left for California to go to a Christian counseling center. The counseling sessions gave us hope and encouragement that with God's help, we could get back to "normal" and have a fresh start.

Some time later, I felt well enough to apply for jobs. During the application process I was often asked, "Have you ever been hospitalized for mental issues?" My answer had to be yes. I had to rise above the stigma of suffering a nervous breakdown. It wasn't easy, but with God's help, within five years I became successful in my line of work. Throughout the following years I even received awards for sales achievements.

But the greatest miracle of all is that God "delivered me from all my fears," as the psalmist David put it (Psalm 34:4). This truly was a miracle of healing. I am forever grateful to the Lord for His healing touch.

I sought the LORD, and He heard me, and delivered me from all my fears. (Psalm 34:4 NKJV)

Adam Neal is enjoying retirement now and continues to be grateful for a peaceful heart and mind.

27

Light House Down the Street

Vernon L. Thompson

"Preacher, we need help. Food, clothes, housing, money—anything would help us." These were the words of two men dressed in rumpled overalls and denim shirts who were standing in my office at Calvary United Methodist Church in Maryland. It was a hot, summer day.

I soon found out they were fishermen who were newly out of work and had been sleeping under a nearby bridge just outside our church doors. After listening to their stories and giving them some groceries and vouchers for lodging, I determined to take their plight before the Annapolis Ministerial Association, of which I was the current president.

The need was obvious. Although each of the six downtown churches in the association had its own assistance program, we needed to unite our efforts if we were going to effectively tackle homelessness and hunger in downtown Annapolis. A task force soon began developing a plan. A makeshift place of respite, which consisted of only six cots, was immediately set up in St. Anne's Episcopal Church's parish house in the center of the city.

The other five churches took turns housing the homeless on their premises, especially during the winter. Three years later, through donations, gifts, and grants, the association purchased an abandoned storefront building with apartments overhead on West Street in downtown Annapolis. It was the ideal location because it was in the midst of the business section, which could provide employment; it was on the main city bus line, which provided easy and affordable transportation; and it had the potential to be expanded. Thus was born Light House, a homeless prevention support center that served fifteen residential clients and provided lunches to people in the community.

There was only one problem: the center was located only two city blocks from a prestigious enclave of stately older homes filled with wealthy owners. Many of these homeowners were also the movers and shakers of Annapolitan life. They claimed the Light House adversely affected property values, that an unwanted clientele was roaming their streets, and that "there were no housing or hunger problems in the capital city of Maryland." So they sued to cancel the project.

Weeks before the case came to trial, we sent prayer appeals not only to the Annapolis churches but also churches around the state. We set up prayer vigils. In the end, the Annapolis Area Ministries won the case.

We planned a mile-long dedication parade down Main Street on a Sunday morning, beginning at St. Anne's Parish House and ending at the Light House. This parade would also publicize the fact that the center was opening and functioning. But we were denied the parade permit because the city said it had no funds for police to monitor the event, which was a city requirement. Again, we sent out a prayer appeal. We prayed for permission to hold the parade so the community could realize that the center was a wonderful and necessary addition to Annapolis.

On Saturday, the day before the dedication, we received a notice from the city saying that adequate funds had been given to cover the cost of police to monitor the parade. Later, we discovered that the same lawyer who had filed the first lawsuit to stop the project had contributed the funds.

At the beginning of this project, I felt that each minister was clothed in the sandals of David the shepherd boy going up against the giant Goliath. There was a vast difference between our dream and our plan. As they say, an effective plan is "SMART," by which I mean Specific, Measurable, Achievable, Relevant to your problem, and includes a Time line. Our dreams were vague longings of the heart that we turned into a plan by faith and prayer. "The battle is the Lord's," as David said (1 Samuel 17:47).

After we successfully completed an $8.4 million fundraising campaign, the Lord graciously blessed the Light House with a new, twenty-four-thousand-square-foot facility with the capacity to house thirty men, fifteen women, and five families with up to twenty children. It also contained a large commercial kitchen. The pantry program began distributing 250 bag lunches each day and 400 bags of groceries each month. The following year, we established the Building Employment Success Training (BEST) program to provide job training and skills that could help residents find sustainable employment and, eventually, permanent housing.

This program truly was the Lord's doing. He made the way for us to go from a six-cot beginning in a parish house lobby to the multimillion-dollar facility supported by the whole community.

The battle is the LORD's, and he will give all of you into our hands.
(1 Samuel 17:47)

Vernon L. Thompson is the former pastor of Calvary United Methodist Church, Annapolis, Maryland. He is a member of the founding board of directors of the Light House Shelter.

28

The All-American Fix

PAULY HELLER

A miracle doesn't have to be extravagant to be nonetheless a miracle—an incident in which God intervenes and does something for which there is no other explanation than "God did this."

I was a full-time stay-at-home mom with eight- and six-year-old boys and a four-year-old daughter. We were involved and busy with homeschooling, soccer practices and games, church fellowship groups and activities, not to mention the frequent marriage communication workshops my husband, Alan, and I often led. We had a large backyard equipped with a swing set and a ten-by-ten-foot sandbox where our kids spent hours of creative playtime.

With two older brothers challenging her constantly, little Jessica worked hard to make her presence felt and her voice heard. She climbed, jumped, ran, dug, and kicked soccer balls right along with Josh and David.

On one occasion, while playing with her brothers, she came to me in tears and presented me with a thumbnail that had broken straight across at the quick, with the break extending partway into the nail bed. Knowing I couldn't trim off the broken part, which ended in a sharp point, without cutting into the tender nail bed, I decided on an All-American fix: a Band-Aid. I wrapped one around her thumb, safely enclosing the broken nail so it wouldn't catch on anything and rip off. Then I gave the finger a magic Mommy kiss, and sent Jessi happily on her way.

What a great fix! What a good Mom! Problem all gone.

Until several days later, when Jessi whined, "Mommy, my thumb hurts!" Her thumb! I had forgotten all about it.

I peeled off the Band-Aid and unveiled the little package of infection my first-aid handiwork had wrought on my daughter. The entire tip of her thumb was inflamed and puffy where the skin had grown around the point of the nail, embedding it in a pus-filled sac. It was bright red and hot to the touch. I drew in a sharp breath, feeling condemned for my neglect and medical malpractice. Poor little Jessi! She was in pain.

I immediately called the doctor's office for advice on what to do. "This is going to require a little minor surgery," the nurse told me. "You can bring your daughter in around four o'clock at the end of the doctor's day, and he'll probably numb the area and cut out the nail. She may need a stitch or two. Till then, you can give her some Tylenol."

It was nearly naptime anyway, so I gave Jessi a spoonful of orange-colored medicine, tucked her into her bottom bunk for a nap, and knelt by the side of her bed to pray for her.

I closed my eyes and found myself on a dusty, crowded village street, reaching out toward Jesus, who I knew was just ahead of me. "Lord Jesus," I began, knowing instantly I had His full, undivided attention. So I talked to Him in my normal voice, not my "prayer voice," as though He were way far away up in heaven (where He usually is), so I have to talk kind of loudly and formally, even in my mind, so He can hear me. But here on this street, He was right there, so I just said to Him, "Lord, Jessica's thumb is really sore, and I don't know what to do. Can you touch her and fix it, please?"

I don't know if I even said "Amen" because He was right there, and when does anyone say "Amen" to a person who's right there in front of you?

I stood up and tiptoed out the door. Jessi was already asleep.

Two hours later, Jessi's voice rang from her room. "Mommy! Mommy! Look! My thumb is all better!" I ran to her room, not sure of what she meant. As I opened her door, Jessi lifted her thumb aloft like a little candle for me to see. "Look, Mommy! Jesus made my thumb all better!"

And surely and truly, He had! Her precious little thumb, totally pink and normal, bore absolutely no evidence of ever having been sore and inflamed; her nail, no longer even split, was wholly restored, as though it had never been broken. We hugged and rejoiced and thanked Jesus for His goodness. Then I called the doctor and cancelled the appointment.

Why did Jesus grant me this intimate moment of immediacy with Him? Why did He allow me to witness firsthand His power to heal my daughter's fingernail, yet twenty-eight years later allow my firstborn son to die from colorectal cancer? Maybe He wanted me to know that in both cases—in the healing and in the home-going—He is always right here.

"And lo, I am with you always, even to the end of the age." (Matthew 28:20)

Pauly Heller is now "Grandma" to David and Jessi's children. She is also coauthor with her husband, Alan, of *The Marital Mystery Tour* (AMFM Press) and, with Alan and Dr. Ed Delph, of *Learning How to Trust…Again* (Destiny Image).

29

New Memories

Carol M.

Our son Zach has always had a lot of friends because of his fun, loving, salesmanlike personality. Fortunately my husband, Tim, and I were always able to be his friends too. As he grew up, he seemed to grow more open with us, regularly opening up for heart-to-heart conversations. Zach even won a business trip to Orlando and, amazingly, chose me, his mother, to go with him. Later he took his dad when he won a trip to Hawaii. That's the way our family was.

One day, not long after Zach was married, he came to me and asked about the way we had disciplined him. When he and his sister were younger, Tim and I tried our best to love and train them well. We certainly didn't do everything perfectly, and we've humbly admitted to many errors, yet we tried to love our children and apply parental discipline with discernment and love. As soon as Zach brought this up, I was confused. He'd never seemed so affected by those types of memories.

He then told me that his wife had prompted him to see a counselor about his past because, according to her, he had abandonment issues and was "unable to cope with life." He felt that she would threaten their marriage if he didn't go to a counselor. When she picked out a counselor, he felt compelled to go.

That day, Zach asked me to go with him to his counseling session. The hesitation and incredible angst I was feeling about this had nothing to do with the counseling itself, but with the topic that seemed to have come up out of the clear blue.

The office was black and dark when we got there. When the counselor arrived and turned on the lights, she told me exactly where to sit and said I couldn't speak a word, ask a question, or seek clarification. I was just to listen. She then began telling me of Zach's internal struggles with the way we disciplined him as a child, and how those things had caused him great damage in his ability to cope.

"You have ruined him," she said to me, continuing on with further statements of how I was a bad influence. She told me that all the encouraging notes I wrote to Zach were unhealthy because "they caused Zach to feel uncomfortable and uneasy."

Yet Zach had thanked me many times for the notes of encouragement and praise. He had written me letters telling me that I was his example. He'd involved me in his life since young adulthood.

This counselor was describing Zach as a person I didn't know. There was no truth in her words. I felt it was all a blatant attack on me.

I wasn't a perfect parent by any means. Yet throughout my adult relationship with Zach, I sought to understand him. I cared about where he was coming from when we discussed past hurts. I'd birthed, raised, and loved him for thirty years! This situation was simply confusing. I felt angry, condemned, and betrayed.

The counselor then told us that neither Tim nor I were to have any contact with Zach or his family. No communication. No letters. No notes of affirmation. No seeing our one-year-old granddaughter. I walked out of the office certain this was the darkest experience I'd ever had.

Driving home, I cried my heart out. I was devastated, angry, and confused. It felt as if my heart had a sword through it and it had been twisted until I could no longer stand the pain.

Tim and I immediately went straight to a Christian counselor and friend named Alan. After hearing our story, Alan wisely said, "This is a *spiritual* battle. Go home, get a prayer team, and start praying." We called and e-mailed a number of friends who graciously agreed to partner with us in prayer for the power of Satan to be broken and for our relationship with Zach to be restored. Meanwhile, we tried to reconcile with Zach and see if we could talk things through. Two times we reached out only to be unpleasantly reminded we were to have no communication with him.

For six months, I cried daily. The pain and loss were deep. I began spending long periods every day reading the Word to get my feet on level ground. As Jesus' presence became my sustenance and His Word my perspective, He reminded me of a time earlier in life when a counselor had said, "The person who has hurt you will come out of it. When they do, have a ready heart to receive them. Otherwise, you'll want to say, 'You owe me because you hurt me.' Let the Holy Spirit keep your heart clean." So I started working on daily forgiving Zach, his wife, and the counselor.

But it still didn't explain the darkness of the situation. After about a year, and through a divine appointment, the Lord led me to a friend who instantly identified the type of psychological counseling Zach had received and which had ensnared him: false memory syndrome. False memory syndrome is a condition in which a person's identity and relationships are affected by memories that are factually wrong but strongly believed. In our case, the counselor led Zach to believe our discipline damaged him for life, and that the only way for him to survive and overcome those memories was for us to be removed. My prayers for Zach now had a target. I prayed for God to heal and restore his *right* and *true* memories back to him.

Two and half years after the awful meeting with Zach's counselor, Tim and I took our annual day trip north to hike and see the beautiful fall trees. At the time, Zach was living in the area, so I said to Tim, "I know we're forbidden to go by Zach's house or to see anyone in their family, but I have to go by and just see his house and where they live."

"I had the same thought," said Tim. So we nervously turned off the main road and proceded slowly down their street. Lo and behold, on the opposite side of the street, a nanny was pushing a stroller with our two granddaughters inside.

"Tim," I said, "turn around and drive slowly past them. I need to see my granddaughters. I promise to duck down and be quiet." We turned around and started back slowly. Just after we drove past the nanny and the two girls, Zach came around the corner on his bike.

"We're busted!" said Tim.

Both of us knew we weren't supposed to be there. We could only wonder what Zach might say or do to us. Zach rode right up to the driver's side of the car. We were both scared out of our minds. Tim rolled the window down just a crack—only enough to talk to Zach. To our amazement, Zach started talking about his new bike—the suspension—and his bike ride.

"Don't you want to come back to the house and come in?" he asked.

We were stunned. Without hesitation, Tim turned the car around. "Lord, help! We need You more than ever now!" we both cried aloud in prayer. We cautiously pulled onto the driveway, got out of the car, and walked into the garage with Zach. His wife and our two granddaughters, Skye and Caylee, were standing there. Before we knew it, Zach turned to his three-year-old Skye and said: "Wouldn't you like Grams [my grandmother name] to read you a story?"

I followed Skye to her bedroom, sat down on her bed—still in shock and fighting back tears—and read her a story. While I was reading the story, Zach appeared. "Skye, don't you want Grams to read you another story?"

Several stories later, I decided to leave because I was uncomfortable, nervous, and unsure of what might happen next. Tim had gone to the car for the same reasons. We were aware that Zach had told us twice that we were to never be at their house. *Did the rules of this game just change?* I wondered.

But Zach stopped me as I was trying to leave, saying he wanted to show me something they had done on their new home. While I was going with him, he looked at me with his smile—all of you mothers know what I mean. I knew it would be okay when I saw that Zach smile.

When we finally left, Tim and I were in shock. We cried and rejoiced as we drove out to see the leaves. We knew that only through our prayers and the prayers of our faithful friends could Zach be set free from Satan and the hands of his counselor.

Zach invited us back into his life as if nothing negative had ever happened. And the Lord answered my prayers. I didn't feel a need to say "You were wrong" or to hold him accountable for my pain. I could have rejected his acceptance, but instead my heart was able to receive it. By the grace of God I was able to move on with a clean heart.

Tim and I never imagined the way the Lord would reconcile us with our son. Zach has encouraged us to visit his family anytime we can. During our visits, Tim, Zach, and I have had heart-to-hearts just as before. We have our son back! And I can only credit the Lord for this complete restoration.

The Lord brings healing and renewal. His power is at work in each of us. He is sovereign in our most painful situations, proving His ways wonderful, complete, and beyond anything we could ever ask or imagine. He truly cares for us and graciously hears and answers our prayers.

"There is hope for your descendants," declares the LORD. "Your children will return to their own land." (Jeremiah 31:17)

Carol M. is a mentor to young women and enjoys swimming and hiking. She and her husband now delight in plentiful visits and vacations with their granddaughters.

30

An Unscathed Mind

Keri Jackson

It was a beautiful, mid-September Saturday morning. My husband, Tom, had just left to take our son, Brady, to his junior high football pregame warm-ups. I planned to meet them an hour later for the game.

As soon as they left, I had one of those coveted Mom moments of sudden peace and quiet in the house. I was all alone in the house because our eldest child, Emily, was off at her first year of college, while our other two teenaged daughters, Whitney and Bethany, were at an overnight cross-country meet. I relaxed into the morning, took a shower, and put on my makeup. I had time to spare. It felt like a day at the spa...until my cell phone rang. It was my neighbor Desiree.

"Well, hi there, Desiree," I said in a cheery voice. "Happy Saturday—"

"No, Keri! Listen to me!" she interrupted. "It's Tom—he's been in an accident!"

Fear gripped me as she continued.

"I was on the road to the high school when I encountered his car coming toward me and stopping only inches from mine. My son Levi cried out, 'Mom! That's Tom's car, and that's Tom slumped over the wheel!' We called 911, and the paramedics are rushing him to the emergency room. You need to leave right now and meet them there!"

God...no...no! Shaking with disbelief and shock, I collected my thoughts so I could function enough to get into the car. Heading down the hill from my neighborhood, I prayed over and over again: *God, please don't take Tom...please don't take Tom...please don't take Tom...*

Paramedics met me at the entrance of the emergency room and directed me to a room on the left. I saw Tom lying on an emergency table surrounded by doctors and nurses working tirelessly to revive him.

Tom had suffered a cardiac arrest. They needed to stabilize his brain immediately through a medicated coma and apply a full-body, twenty-four-hour ice blanket over his unconscious form. The coma coupled with the applied ice would be crucial if he had any chance of escaping brain damage—that is, if he survived.

I called the key people who were in charge of our kids at their various activities, so they could tell them what had happened. Then I walked down to the waiting room of the ICU. I landed on a chair in an emotional heap. From there, I called my dearest friend, Beth, who in turn notified our friends, church, and extended family to ask everyone to start praying for Tom.

Never before had I leaned on Jesus like I did that day. The fears of becoming a single mom, managing a household alone, and raising a son and three daughters to full adulthood were daunting.

As word began to spread, the ICU waiting room became a house of prayer and support. By nightfall there were forty or so people there to love, support, and pray for Tom and our family. As one person left, another would come. Our church was truly being the church to us. Pastor Maddox never left our side. Emily's closest friends came to the hospital to support her. Whitney and Bethany were prayed over on their athletic bus, and then they rode to the hospital along with Moms in Prayer families. Brady was offered an invitation to sleep over at a close friend's home, a welcome diversion from fear of losing his dad.

Additional families organized meals to be sent to the hospital in the following days, and our pantry at home soon was filled to overflowing.

Our physical, mental, and spiritual needs were met at every turn. We lacked nothing, and peace ensued amid the stress of Tom's condition.

Later that evening, I was finally allowed to see Tom. I walked into the room where he lay in a coma. I was completely unprepared to see him hooked up to all the equipment, with tubes down his throat.

With a Bible from the waiting room in hand, I turned to Psalm 139, knowing if God created Tom in secret, He was also fully aware what was happening within his body right now. *This will be Your story, God,* I prayed. I took comfort in the precious thoughts that God had toward Tom, believing Tom's days were ordained and written in God's book of life before one of them came to pass.

Later, back in the waiting room, when a woman sitting beside me learned of my husband's story, she said, "I can't believe how calm and peaceful you are." I told her I couldn't explain it either. I just knew God was going to care for us, and I trusted Him.

After forty-eight hours, it was time for Tom to come out of the medicated coma. Despite ICU guidelines that only two people could be in his room at a time, I asked his attending nurse, whom we'd found out was a Romanian Christian, for permission for all the friends and family currently in the waiting room to come stand beside Tom's bed. She not only agreed to this, but she also asked if she could have the honor of leading them in prayer for him. As we surrounded his bedside, I could sense each heart surrendered to God, praying for His will to be done. I clung to the prayers spoken in faith. "In Jesus' name, we ask that Tom be protected from any ill effects as he wakes. Amen."

As Tom began waking up and stabilizing, he showed signs of confusion about why and how he'd landed in the hospital. We continued to have conversations with him, and the Tom we knew and loved prior to the incident came back. The paramedics told us that they rarely see this. Of the 5 percent that survive a cardiac arrest, most are left with varying degrees of brain damage.

Even though Tom would need two stents and an implanted medical device, this was a small price to pay for mental wholeness coming through what cardiologists call a widow-maker event.

Through Tom's most tentative hours and in the nights of my personal unrest, the Lord spoke and reminded me that He is the great *I Am*, and that He had Tom in the palm of His hand.

I've since found out about many ways God orchestrated Tom's deliverance that day. Desiree, our neighbor, was providentially on the scene of the accident. Onlookers with CPR certification and equipment stopped to help. Paramedics had delayed their travel for another cup of coffee, which put them only two minutes from the scene. The closest hospital was the one that pioneered the ice blanket treatment for brain stabilization post trauma. Finally, Tom's second transfer to another hospital put him into the hands of one of the most respected electrocardiologists in the country. In everything, God's timing was perfect.

Lord, may we never forget and always be reminded that in life or in death You never leave us alone. You always provide. You are always faithful!

The verse the Lord gave Tom while in the hospital, and which has become our life's charge, is Psalm 50:15:

Call on me in the day of trouble; I will deliver you, and you will honor me.

As Interior Design Consultant, **Keri Jackson** seeks to bring change and hope to her client's lives. She has three daughters and recently lost her only son to a tragic car accident. She and her husband are on an unexpected journey to redeem what was lost for His eternal purposes.

31

Thin-Glass Prayers

Marty Trammell

"Who do we know who has any money?" My young wife, Linda, dropped her head and slid into the green vinyl dinette chair, tearing a clump of yellowed foam from a rip in its side.

"No one, I guess."

"Then what are we going to do? Move back into an apartment?"

I glanced away from her tears, dragging my eyes around the duplex we were renting from a friend. It had started to feel like home.

"Are you sure we can't squeeze more from our budget?" Her warm, brown eyes repeated the look I'd seen many times in the past month.

"Well, we could take food stamps; we do qualify. Maybe we should change our minds and sign up. It would save us the amount we need to pay for the rent increase."

She looked around the duplex as if for the last time. "No, they're meant for the poor, and we're not starving. There's got to be another way."

I closed the sliding-glass door behind me and watched her as she lowered her head. Thin glass separated our prayers.

Faded, caramel-colored deck paint peeled beneath my shoes

as I stepped toward the large Styrofoam computer-packaging container Linda had pulled from the neighborhood recycling bin. She'd turned it into a sandbox for our two-year-old son, Justin, and his baby brother, Christopher. I sat with Justin on the worn edge of the box.

"Daddy, watch this!" Justin lifted a small plastic block, revealing a perfect square of sand.

"Daddy, this is the house where Mary and Jophus put baby Jesus." Justin loved the deck and the sandbox. He'd play for hours in his make-believe world of sand castles and Hot Wheels. As I watched him play, hopeless thoughts of moving back into a smaller apartment fell like grains of sand between my fingers.

The following weeks faded into the gray clouds of fall. The raise in rent approached. The salary scale at the small Christian college where I taught had frozen because of dwindling enrollment. No answer there. The youth pastor position at the small country church we'd decided to serve could only provide enough to cover the gas expenses. No answer there. The secretarial position my wife had left to stay at home with our sons provided no option for work at home. No answer there. Narnia's "always winter, but never Christmas" punctuated my thoughts.

One day my wife asked me, "Guess who called this morning after you left for work? Doreen."

"Your friend from high school? How's she doing?" I noticed a small tear as Linda turned toward the kitchen.

"She's fine."

I set down a stack of college writing papers and put my arms around my wife. Her shoulders shook.

"She said we shouldn't be renting, that it's smarter to buy a house. She and Kenny just bought one in Seattle."

"Honey, she doesn't know our situation. I'm sure she wouldn't have said anything if she'd known we were struggling."

I stared over her shoulder at the butcher-block countertop. "We can't get a loan, we can't buy a house, we can't afford the rent, we can't—" I let go and slumped into a dinette chair, hoping she wouldn't see in my eyes the fears that plagued my thoughts. There was nothing else to do but finally force myself to make the decision to move into an apartment or leave the ministry to earn more money.

Linda picked up a sippy cup Justin had left in the kitchen. "What do you want for dinner?" Her words trailed off and we drifted into an almost silent evening.

The next morning a pulsating phone ring shattered the Saturday-morning stillness. I rolled over and lifted the receiver.

"Hi, is this Marty? This is Marilyn Dorn, Doreen's mom. Can we talk for a moment?" I sat up and stuffed a pillow behind my head.

"Sure."

"I was wondering if you could do me a favor? I invest in real estate here in Seattle, and I've done quite well. I was thinking about expanding down the I-5 corridor into Salem, Oregon."

"Okay."

"Well, I was wondering if you could find two or three starter homes for me. I could use the additional investments. I'd remodel them and sell them for a profit."

"Okay. I'm sure I could talk to an agent and mail you some pictures and descriptions. Is that what you're looking for?"

"That would be perfect. Are you sure it wouldn't be too much to ask?" I slid lower into the bed.

"No, we'd be glad to help."

"Okay. Thanks. I'll call you back in a couple of weeks." As I set the phone in its cradle, I couldn't help but wonder why Doreen's mom, Marilyn, would call two days after Doreen got in touch with my wife. I'd never met either of them, and Linda hadn't seen Marilyn in several years.

"Who was it?" Linda's barely open eyes focused slowly.

"Doreen's mom wants us to send her pictures of a few houses in Salem. She invests in real estate now."

"Real estate? Why did she call us?"

"Something about the I-5 corridor and rising house prices. Did Doreen say anything about this?"

"No, but that's kind of weird, isn't it?"

I sat straight up and threw the covers back. "Linda, what if she wants us to help with the remodels? And what if she lets us rent from her or live in the homes until they sell? What if…"

Linda sat up too.

The next week I mailed three sets of pictures and descriptions of the fixer-uppers we'd found. And Linda and I prayed. Not just our three-meals-a-day prayers, but during nearly every break in our routines.

Three days later Marilyn called. As she went through the normal greetings, my mind raced. Just the sound of her voice filled my head with hope.

Please, let us fix these up for her, I prayed as she finished her hellos. I glanced at Linda, who was reading to Chris and Justin. Her head was bowed.

"Well, Marty, I would like to discuss something with you, if now's a good time."

"Now's a great time, Mrs. Dorn. We're just playing with the boys."

"Oh, okay. Well, the reason I wanted to talk with you, Marty, is that—I don't want to offend you in any way, but I know you're both serving the Lord and well, like I said earlier, I've made some money in Seattle flipping houses. And lately I've been helping young couples in the ministry get into their first homes. So when Doreen told me you were still renting, I checked up on your salary at the college. I hope that's okay."

"Sure. Anyone can get a copy of the pay scale. I'm not sure I understand why, though." I stretched the phone cord over the table and sat at the dinette. *Please, Lord, if we could only help her remodel these homes and have a place for Justin and Chris to play,* I prayed.

"Well, looking at your salary and the loan amount you'd be able to qualify for, I'm figuring you'll need at least $14,000 to get into one of the homes you sent descriptions of."

"Yes, around $14,000. But we've already tried to qualify for various home loans, Mrs. Dorn. We can't—"

"Oh, I know," Mrs. Dorn cut in. "Doreen told me about you and Linda the same day I was praying about finding another young couple to help out. It's not a loan, Marty. I want to *give* you the money."

"*Give* us the money?"

"Well, if that's all right with you, that is."

"Um, all right with me? You said you want to *give* us $14,000?" Startled, Linda put Chris on the carpet and came to stand beside my chair.

"Mrs. Dorn, I don't know what to say. This is more than we ever hoped for. I don't know what to say. Thank you! Thank you! What would be the next step?" I asked as I stood and put my arm around Linda's waist. I whispered, "She wants to help us buy one of the homes we found."

Linda and I sat at our table that night poring over the same budget we'd gone over countless times. The worn pages where we'd written figures and erased them over and over were the same. Only this time we penciled in $14,000 on a line that before had been empty. The line-item description read, "Our Home."

The day we signed papers, we wrote a thank-you card to Mrs. Dorn. As we opened the door to the mailbox to send it, a letter sat waiting. Linda reached for it.

"It's from Marilyn!" she said, tearing the end off the envelope.

Dear Marty and Linda, I can't tell you how happy it made me to be able to help a young couple continue in the ministry. I've enclosed a check as a housewarming gift...

"A house-warming gift? She just helped us buy the house. Why would she send a house warming gift?" I asked.

"I don't know." Linda smiled warmly. "But do you think we can do anything with a thousand dollars?"

I waited patiently for the LORD to help me, and he turned to me and heard my cry. He lifted me out of the pit of despair, out of the mud and the mire. He set my feet on solid ground and steadied me as I walked along. (Psalm 40:1-2 NLT)

Marty Trammell enjoys the outdoors, reading, and serving with his amazing wife, Linda, and family and friends at Corban University, Valley Baptist Church, and the website redeemingrelationships.com.

32

Twenty Years of Wondering

Wanda MacLean

It was eight o'clock in the evening in Budapest, Hungary, in the fall of 1994. I'd just settled into my seat inside the sliding doors of the subway. It felt good to have a reprieve from the cold, autumn air. I had five minutes to indulge my people-watching habit before my final stop. There was a pretty blonde woman with a sweet little girl sitting across from me. I thought, *Are you really a blonde or do you dye your hair?* To my surprise, her voice interrupted my silent inquiry.

"Excuse me. Do you speak English?" She sounded American. Then to my greater surprise, she asked, "Is your name Wanda?"

I desperately struggled to recognize this stranger.

"It's me, Cindy Larson," she said.

My mind raced back to 1974 when I first met Cindy in high school. After that, we entered the same nursing program and went to our OB (obstetrics) rotation together. Abortions had just become legal, but our nursing school avoided talking about it. We weren't even allowed onto the hospital floor where abortion patients were staying. One day, however, our nursing instructor led just the two of us, Cindy and me, into a secluded room.

"I could lose my job for showing you this," she said.

Cindy and I found ourselves standing above a sterile, stainless-steel counter. Lying in the middle was a little baby with her hand touching her cheek. Her mother had just had a saline abortion while five months pregnant, and this was her lifeless little girl.

"I could never have an abortion!" Cindy exclaimed.

It was a powerful and sad moment for the both of us.

Cindy and I soon became friends. She told me she had a church upbringing but had stopped attending since college. I began praying for her walk with the Lord. One day the Lord gave me an opportunity to share my testimony with her during one of our lunch breaks.

"I admire you for your faith," she said, "but I'm not ready to do that. I'm having a lot of fun right now."

I continued to pray for her. One year later, we sat in a park and I shared the gospel with her again. Her response was warm, but no different than the last time.

"Thanks, but I'm not ready for this," she said.

Now, twenty years later in a city of 2.2 million people, we found ourselves ascending a steep elevator from the subway to bustling Budapest's Moscow Square.

I told her that I was a missionary, and my purpose in Hungary was to tell people about the hope of Jesus.

"What are you doing in Budapest, Cindy?" I asked on the elevator steps.

"My husband and I just arrived as new missionaries," she said. "Wanda, I accepted Christ about one month after we last met. I've always wanted to find you and thank you for sharing the gospel with me."

One week later, Cindy and I met at my favorite coffee shop, and she told me more of her story. She told me the sad news that she'd had two abortions after our time in nursing school. I could only imagine the torment she experienced after that, and yet this is what drew her into the forgiving arms of Jesus, where she experienced His redeeming peace.

God let me see the answer to prayer for Cindy's salvation twenty years after the fact and nine thousand miles away from where it all began. But, truly, this change didn't start with my encounter with Cindy in nursing school, but years before when she was skillfully wrought in her mother's womb.

You formed my inward parts; you knitted me together in my mother's womb. I praise you, for I am fearfully and wonderfully made. Wonderful are your works; my soul knows it very well. (Psalm 139:13-14 ESV)

Wanda MacLean served as a full-time missionary with Cru for thirty-seven years and touched the lives of many through her love for people and gregarious personality. She passed away from cancer in 2014.

33

10:15

JODI CARLSON

I have insomnia. Not just last night or for the past two weeks. Not in the past two months or even in the past two years. All thirty-six years of my life, since birth, sleep has not come naturally for me. Bleak nights of anxiety and despair have been unwelcome companions of mine. Doctors' offices and every kind of medication have been part of my life story. All of the medical professionals I've ever visited were perplexed. Finally, when I was twenty-two, I saw a sleep specialist. His diagnosis? Primary idiopathic insomnia.

"What does that mean?" I asked, eager to finally have a name for my nemesis.

"It means there's no medical, psychological, or environmental explanation for your insomnia," he said. "And it means you've had it since birth."

Gee, thanks, Captain Obvious, I thought.

The unfortunate thing about long-term insomnia is that it's not isolated to your nights. Rather, it affects your entire being: your body, your spirit, and, most importantly, your mind. Over time, with some added oomph from my genes, I came to know insomnia's dreaded brother and sister: anxiety and depression. These three have come to form a triangular beast in my life—one I'm not proud of but that I've come to accept just as a person must accept the color of his or her skin.

I could tell story after story of my countless prayers regarding sleep. I cried out to God to just let me sleep, only to lie awake hour after hour with ever-increasing anxiety that tomorrow would be a horrible day and, of course, drowning in panic that something was deeply wrong with me. Misery, hopelessness, and isolation consumed me. It seemed as if God didn't care and no one would ever understand.

One month, I was on the verge of collapse and at risk of losing my job because I couldn't function. I'd been at this spot before, and had, in fact, quit my dream job as a magazine editor when I was twenty-four-years old and moved halfway across the country to live with my parents in order to get healthy and rebuild. Eight years later, I again had a job I loved and was blessed with a supportive community of believers around me.

But the vicious tri-beast—anxiety, depression, and insomnia—was consuming me. It was all I could do to get through each day and collapse on my bed again at night, only to be robbed once more of the one thing that could restore me. My eyes were hollow. My heart was numb. I echoed my tiny prayers over and over again: "Help me, God. You're all I've got. Deliver me."

I'd learned over the years from Job 13:15 that my pain doesn't imply that God has weakness. As Job put it, "Though he slay me, yet will I hope in him" (Job 13:15). God is not limited. Rather, *my* perspective is limited. I am merely a human confined to linear thought. I am not privy to God's perspective, so who am I to judge Him and put Him in a box labeled "Mean"?

On this particular night, I reached for a book on my bedside stand. I was in the middle of *Hinds Feet on High Places*, a beautiful allegory about Much Afraid (a character) and the different terrain the Shepherd would lead her through, teaching her lessons each step of the way. I also simultaneously reached for my iPod. I'd never put those two together before. Usually I would either read or I would listen to relaxing music to try to get my mind off of the fact I wasn't sleeping. But on this night, I reached for both. It was around ten fifteen.

I opened my book and began to read. This particular section was about Much Afraid walking through a forest, observing the trees and listening to the birds. Then the strangest thing happened. I began to hear birds. It was a soft, beautiful chirping—a delicate melody of praise. I heard rushing water, just as Much Afraid walked along a streambed. I stopped. I looked up at my bedroom wall. *What was happening? Where was I?*

After a dazed moment, reality hit me. My iPod was on shuffle and the song that just happened to play in the very moment I started the forest scene with Much Afraid was a nature tune, a song of wildlife sounds I had downloaded from a CD labeled "Relax into Sleep."

Tears immediately welled up and overflowed. God cared about me so much that He put these two things together in that moment to minister to my spirit and remind me of my hope in Him. It was completely beautiful and humbling. As Much Afraid was learning how to trust her Shepherd, I was doing the same. God cared. He loved me. He would see me through.

The next day, I was just as exhausted as I'd been every day the previous month, but I had hope deep within my soul. My mom called to check in on me, as she had been consistently tracking with me in my misery.

"Did you fall asleep early last night, say around ten fifteen?" she asked.

My forehead wrinkled. "Well, no," I replied. "But God spoke to me at that time as He never has before."

"What happened?" she asked.

I told her the story and she began to weep. "That was when I prayed out loud for the devil to get away from you," she said. "I prayed for God to wrap His two palms around your head, to calm your mind, to hold and comfort you."

I still don't understand all the suffering I've had to endure as a result of the insomnia–anxiety–depression beast in my life. But I do know the triune God with an intimacy I can't explain. No matter what I go through, I know that I am His and that He will remain my God, my Shepherd, and my forever Hope.

Though [God] slay me, yet will I hope in him. (Job 13:15)

Jodi Carlson is a freelance writer and editor living in the beautiful Pacific Northwest. She's written scripts for Luis Palau's radio broadcasts, published many magazine articles, and collaborated on Dr. Kristin Beasley's *Who Do You Think You Are?*

34

Heaven Invading Surabaya

JOSUÉ RAMIREZ

One day, when my friends Julie, Moush, and I were on a mission trip in Surabaya, Indonesia, we had a few hours to spare. Desiring that God would move powerfully through us with His compassion and love, we went to Surabaya's main village store and bought a lot of food and candy. We then asked God to tell us where to go.

The Holy Spirit speaks in creative and mysterious ways. As we were praying for direction about who He wanted us to love, we felt Him bring to our minds the word *chicken*. *What does that mean?* we asked ourselves. We continued walking through the streets of Surabaya and asking God to show us where He wanted us to go. Suddenly we saw a chicken walking down the sidewalk.

With our bags of candy and food in hand, the three of us followed the chicken as it walked along. The chicken turned into a dark alley, so we followed it down there. When we came to the other side of the alley, we found ourselves in the courtyard of a small Muslim *kampung* neighborhood, which is similar to a slum.

As we entered the *kampung*, twenty children and their parents came out to the courtyard to meet us. We started giving them the food and candy we'd bought. No one in the *kampung* spoke

English, and yet we found a way to communicate, asking if anyone had any sickness or injuries so we could pray for healing.

An old lady came forward. Sitting in a chair in front of us, she looked at us and pointed to her knees and then to a spot on her back. Believing God wanted to move in compassion and love toward this woman, we prayed for her.

After a short, minute-long prayer, the woman stood up and started jumping around. Jesus had completely healed her knees and back! She hugged and kissed me on the cheek, and for the next hour she was jumping up and down with joy.

Right after that healing, five more ladies with similar knee and back injuries lined up for prayer. As my team and I prayed, we saw God touch and heal each of their injuries.

The neighborhood life erupted, and the ladies started taking us to others in the *kampung* who needed prayer for healing. A few men had shoulder and arm injuries from hard labor. Jesus touched and healed every man's injury.

Heaven invaded this neighborhood! It was as if the pages from the book of Acts had come alive in this little compound. For two hours, we celebrated and jumped around with the village children. At the time, it was hard to explain to them who had healed them. The next day, we went back to the *kampung* with a translator.

Through our translator, the first lady we prayed for with severe knee and back pain told us she'd been in pain for many years, and it had always robbed her of a good night's sleep. She went to doctors and took medicine, but nothing worked. Then she told us she had slept well the night before with no pain whatsoever. For the first time in years, all her pain was gone.

Through our translator, we asked her, "Who do you think healed you?"

She pointed at us and said the people believed we had "powers from the sky."

We explained it wasn't us—it wasn't Josué, Julie, or Moush. It was Jesus, the living Son of God in heaven. The people knew the name of Jesus from the Koran. When the lady heard this, she started to tear up.

She wanted prayer again, fearing the pain might come back. But we told her through our translator that our Jesus in heaven had completely healed her and that He was showing her how much He loves her. With endless tears coming down her face, she told us, "Thank you for coming to pray."

Throughout the rest of our trip, we continued to follow up with this neighborhood. For security reasons, we sensitively and carefully shared the good news individually with each person who had been touched by the love of the Father through healing. It was our Father's love and compassion that had healed them, and we wanted to give Him all the glory.

[Jesus] sent them out to proclaim the kingdom of God and to heal the sick. (Luke 9:2)

Josué Ramirez is passionate about pandas, Jesus, evangelism, healing, and revival. He trains young adults in missions and discipleship.

35

Secrets No More

John Warton

My wife and I have four children. All of them are grown, more or less, but our youngest has always been the most willful. She's a strong, brave young woman, and self-reliant to a fault. Despite a youth that was full of teaching and the positive examples of her elder siblings, she began to live with her boyfriend. It should have been no surprise to us that she didn't want us to know where.

We knew she was somewhere on the other side of the city, but our only contact was an occasional smartphone call she would initiate when she had some calling credit. After months of praying, her refusal of our invitations, and of having almost no contact with her, I finally came to a point of desperation. I couldn't tolerate this any longer.

Rather than filing a missing-persons report with the police, hiring a private investigator, or roaming the streets of the city hoping to see her, her car, or her childhood dog, Annie, I decided to seek help by praying that God would reconnect us.

I approached two groups of men in my church: the elder board, of which I was a member, and my small group that met each week. It may sound as if confessing to these men the fact I didn't even know where my daughter was living required considerable humility, but it didn't. I simply wanted to find her. I explained the situation to both groups and asked them to pray with my wife and me that God would allow us to make contact with her.

To the best of our ability, we mixed our prayers with faith and submission. We believed that God could make this happen in a moment—or disallow it as part of His larger plans for her or us. We asked specifically and in His name (John 14:13).

Nothing happened. A week went by, and there was no impromptu visit or phone call. We prayed on. Then Saturday evening of the second week, my wife and I had finished dinner and were about to start a movie when the phone rang. The call was from a local number we didn't recognize. Nonetheless, I answered.

A middle-aged woman was on the other line, asking if we owned a dog named Annie. I informed the woman that Annie was our dog, but our daughter was keeping her now. Apparently Annie had wandered into her yard. When the woman brought her inside, she found the nametag that listed our phone number.

After taking the woman's phone and address, I called our daughter. She didn't answer. After leaving a voice message saying that Annie had wandered away but I knew where to find her, I called our daughter's boyfriend, who was working nights in a pizzeria. Somehow in the noise of the shop and all the activity, he heard the ring and had the time to answer. I relayed the same message about Annie, telling him I knew where to find her. He promised to call our daughter.

Just moments later my wife felt we should retrieve Annie ourselves. So I called the woman to tell her we were coming. After a drive across town, Annie's happy bark and jump assured the kind lady that we were indeed her owners. But before we could drive away, my phone rang. It was our daughter.

She told us she was out with friends looking for Annie on foot and was so thankful for my call. I told her that her mom and I had picked Annie up and had her in our car. She was effusive in her gratitude and told us to meet her at an intersection just two blocks away.

Thirty seconds later, we were together hugging, crying, laughing, and playing with a very happy dog. There were apologies for being so reclusive, promises of being together more often, and invitations to dinner at the house where she was staying.

Within two weeks, God not only answered my specific request, but did so in a much larger way than my wife and I ever imagined. We were able to reconnect with our daughter in a way that showed our concern for what was really important to her: Annie. Nothing—not even her boyfriend at the time—was as important to her as Annie. Moreover, God had worked in our daughter's heart so that she recognized her offenses toward us, and she was truly sorry. The love we had for each other was reaffirmed. It was a beautiful time. And more than just making a phone connection or learning where she lived, we were face-to-face and reunited in heart. It was all a gift of God, an answer to prayer, and something we couldn't have engineered ourselves even if we'd spotted her car in a driveway or received a report identifying her whereabouts.

To my surprise, this was just the beginning of God's answer to our prayers. In the next several months, we did reconnect with our daughter on a regular basis. In discussions over meals, we learned for the first time some of the justifications she felt for turning her back on Christian values. When she became pregnant, we were allowed to help her. Before the birth of her baby, we were able to assist her and her boyfriend in obtaining their own house. And two years later, he asked our permission to marry her. Our families gathered for a Christian wedding that we always remember with joy.

[Jesus said,] "I will do whatever you ask in my name, so that the Father may be glorified in the Son." (John 14:13)

John Warton served five years in the US Army. Following language school and special warfare training, he was sent to Vietnam in 1969. After his tours of duty, John married and entered business in Chicago. He and his wife have four children and twelve grandchildren.

36

My Shortest Prayer

Greg Strannigan

Several years ago I experienced a health crisis. I woke up one morning and every muscle ached. My arms, legs, back—I was stiff and sore all over. The next day was worse. If you've ever had a charley horse, you have an idea of what it felt like, only it was nonstop. It was painful to move. Getting out of bed was an ordeal. My wife's love language is hiking, and I live a pretty active lifestyle. No more.

I discovered that when a person experiences neuro-muscular issues, he gets the attention of the medical community in a hurry. The neurologist didn't waste any time running tests. She pulled out a needle—a *long* needle—and stuck it into my right quadriceps. She said, "Try to lift your leg while I press down against it."

"Okay," I said, and dutifully obeyed.

"You've got a high threshold of pain," she noted.

Honestly, it didn't feel any worse than my new normal. I pointed that fact out to her.

Her diagnosis didn't explain the origin of my symptoms. The best guess was multiple sclerosis, Lyme disease, or ALS (amyotrophic lateral sclerosis).

At this point, my wife started praying Psalm 41:1-3 for me:

Blessed are those who have regard for the weak; the LORD delivers them in times of trouble. The LORD protects and preserves them—they are counted among the blessed in the land—he does not give them over to the desire of their foes. The LORD sustains them on their sickbed and restores them from their bed of illness.

Soon afterward, I met with a neurosurgeon who was confident and self-assured. "You've got cervical stenosis, and I can fix it," he announced.

Apparently, arthritic build-up of calcium was pinching my spinal cord in all the vertebrae in my neck. Instead of being smooth, my spinal cord looked like a Tootsie Roll, compressed into segments.

"I can't go in through the front of the neck," he said. "It's more precise, but it fuses the vertebrae together. All of your vertebrae are involved, and you'd have no range of motion to turn your head. I'll go in through the back and perform a cervical laminectomy. It will clean out the arthritis."

I knew that he was going on vacation to Hawaii in two days, so I figured surgery would be scheduled when he got back home. He threw me for a loop when he said, "We're going to operate tomorrow."

"Why the rush?" I wanted to know.

"You have no protection in your neck. If you were to fall down, you could be paralyzed. I wouldn't risk it. I'll clear my calendar if you clear yours," he said.

After a neurosurgery that lasted almost five hours, I awoke and felt great. The muscle pain was so much better that I got released from the hospital the same day. Before I left, the neurosurgeon said, "You don't need a cervical collar or a neck brace because I went in through the back and those items wouldn't do any good. Just don't do any heavy lifting or kickboxing."

It was like I was given a new life. I felt so good. To celebrate, my lovely wife, Shawn, took me out of town on a getaway to spend the night in a historic hotel. On the way, we hiked several trails to see waterfalls. At the hotel, we checked into our room and I schlepped our luggage up three levels to the top floor.

After dinner, we went back to the room. My neck began to tighten up. *Maybe it's from all the exercise*, I thought. I started having intense muscle spasms. I couldn't find a position that provided relief. I walked to a wing chair and sat down.

"I feel like I ripped a stitch," I told my wife. She checked the stitches on the back of my neck, and they were intact. What I didn't know (but had felt) was the muscle spasms had ripped an interior stitch.

Something didn't feel quite right. I tried moving my right hand, and it wouldn't move. I tried moving my right leg, and it wouldn't move. "I can't move my right hand and my right leg. I think I'm having a stroke," I told Shawn.

"I'm calling 911."

She sounded calm, but I knew she must be frantic.

"That's a good idea," I agreed.

While she was on the phone, I tried moving my left leg. It wouldn't move either. I realized that it probably wasn't a stroke. Finally, I tried moving my left hand. It too remained motionless.

The experience was surreal. I tried bearing down and concentrating, and I focused all of my attention on willing my legs and my arms to respond. Nothing. No pain...no sensation whatsoever.

It was becoming increasingly difficult to breathe. I've been an ambulance driver, and I realized that my life was slipping away. I was dying.

I felt bad for my poor wife, but I was okay with the prospect of meeting Jesus sooner rather than later. My thought was, *If I'm going to die, it's going to be with praises on my lips.* So, I started singing praise and worship songs softly to myself.

Soon after that, paramedics burst into the room. They took

my vitals and gave me oxygen. It made breathing easier, and I figured that I might survive. But my thought was that I'd rather be with the Lord in heaven.

The paramedics strapped me to a backboard and tied my head down really tight (it was the only thing I could actually feel.) The elevator was antique, and wasn't big enough to fit the stretcher. The emergency personnel carried me down three flights of stairs, loaded me into the ambulance, and drove to a local urgent care center.

I found myself in a waiting room at the hospital. It sounded like there was a room full of people, but I couldn't move my head to see. I squinted at the fluorescent lights, which weren't helping my headache. And then I heard the voice of God. It wasn't loud or overwhelming, just a small voice that asked, "Why haven't you prayed for yourself?" *Good question*, I thought. My prayer was as short as it was desperate. "Help me, Lord," I whispered under my breath. And God, in His own unique way, acted on my behalf.

I hadn't had feeling in my fingers for several months, but suddenly I could feel the fingers of my left hand. I tried moving my left arm, and to my amazement it moved! It wasn't strapped down, so I began to wave it around and proclaimed triumphantly to anyone who was there to listen, "I can move my left arm! Check it out!"

Next the left leg. Same thing. I could feel it. I wriggled my toes. Right leg, right arm—the paralysis left in the reverse order that it came. Each time I tried moving a body part, I succeeded, and I let everyone in the ER know.

I was in the process of being prepped for a Life Flight helicopter to the city where we lived, about sixty miles away. But a check on my vitals showed that they had stabilized, so instead I was whisked by ambulance to the local hospital.

We arrived in the parking lot about midnight. Several friends were there waiting. They took Shawn under their wing. One woman, the wife of my general practitioner, told Shawn, "I believe Greg is going to be okay. God gave me this scripture." And she proceeded to read Psalm 41:1-3—the exact same one Shawn had prayed for me during my initial diagnosis.

I was glad to see my neurosurgeon when he walked into the hospital room. He'd been there for the surgery; he'd know what the problem was and what needed to done. An MRI revealed a hematoma (blood clot) more than seven centimeters in diameter pressing on my spinal cord. Bleeding into the spinal cord is a worst-case medical scenario, but it explained the symptoms: paralysis, inability to breathe, vital signs shutting down.

The doctor performed emergency surgery, evacuated the blood clot, and sutured the broken blood vessel. After another four-hour-plus surgery, I left the hospital grateful to be alive but unaware of how extraordinary it was to be mobile.

At the doctor's office the following day, he explained, "You should either be dead or paralyzed. People just don't come back from something like that." He added, "The Big Guy must not be done with you."

Shawn asked, "How did Greg get motion when he was at urgent care?"

"It was the steroids he was given," the doctor surmised.

"He wasn't given *anything* in the ER," my lovely bride noted.

"Well, that's another miracle," the doctor concluded.

I don't pretend to understand prayer, healing, and the ways of God. Prayer isn't magic—it's not a formula. There is so much I don't know about prayer; it's a mystery. But one thing I know is this: Prayer can bring an extra dispensation of the grace of God. Even more than that, it expresses our dependence on Him. If the essence of sin is living independently of God, prayer is the opposite of that.

The shortest and most effective prayer I've ever prayed was simply, "Help me, Lord."

Blessed are those who have regard for the weak; the LORD *delivers them in times of trouble. The* LORD *protects and preserves them— they are counted among the blessed in the land—he does not give them over to the desire of their foes. The* LORD *sustains them on their sickbed and restores them from their bed of illness. (Psalm 41:1-3)*

Greg Strannigan has been a pastor for thirty-five years. He has traveled the world and seen God do amazing things. He says he's blessed with four of the cutest grandchildren on the planet.

37

The Wild Pig

Mercy Ciniraj

My grandmother Eliyamma grew up in a heavily forested area in the state of Kerala, India. Her family was religious but hadn't been taught what it means to have a living relationship with Jesus Christ. Child marriage was common in India at the time, so at the age of thirteen she married a man named Mathai.

Eliyamma and Mathai lived with her family in their mud house in the forest. They had no electricity or running water, and there wasn't a local market to buy food. Her father and Mathai worked hard to reclaim the forest for their small farm, where they cultivated coffee and spices such as pepper and cardamom.

Because the family had no pipes to get suitable drinking water to their house or even a well nearby, it was part of the women's daily chores to fetch water from the river.

One day, when Eliyamma was twenty-seven years old, she walked down to the river to fill up her water pot. As she bent over the water's edge, a wild pig charged out of the underbrush and brutally attacked her. She fought back, using the water pot as a defensive shield and weapon to swing at the pig's head.

But as they fought, the wild pig became even more enraged and fierce. His sharp teeth ripped her legs and arms. Eliyamma knew her life was in jeopardy when blood began to flow profusely from her torn body. She cried out for help, but no one was nearby.

Suddenly a man appeared out of nowhere. He drove the pig away and then knelt down beside Eliyamma to tend to her wounds. When his hands touched the torn places on her body, she was immediately healed.

Still in shock, Eliyamma's eyes grew wide with astonishment as she saw the palms of the man's hands. They were nail-scarred; He carried the markings of crucifixion. Reverence and awe filled her heart. Only one response came to mind as she recognized who attended her. She prostrated herself on the ground and said, "My Lord and my God!"

It was but a moment that she was face down in the soil, which was damp with river water mingled with blood. When she slowly raised her head, her Rescuer had disappeared.

After this dramatic incident, Eliyamma had an insatiable hunger to know more about Jesus. She accepted Him as her personal Savior and, as a result of her testimony, her entire family believed and received Jesus Christ as their Lord and Savior.

In their lifetimes, Eilyamma and Mathai had a total of sixty-seven children, grandchildren, and great-grandchildren.

Being one of them, I grew up knowing Jesus as my Lord and Savior. I married a man named Paul who, though Muslim by birth, accepted Jesus Christ as his personal Savior and Lord on his twenty-first birthday while he was studying at a university. Now we are winning souls for Christ.

My grandfather, Mathai, went home to be with the Lord when Eliyamma was sixty-two. Thirty-nine years later, Jesus took Eliyamma home when she was 101 years old. Up until that day, she eagerly awaited being with her Rescuer face-to-face, and she devoted her life to studying the Bible, praying for others, and glorifying her Lord as His living witness.

"The Lord is my light and my salvation—whom shall I fear?" (Psalm 27:1)

Mercy Ciniraj, copyrighted material from Paul Ciniraj Ministries, http://pciniraj.wordpress.com. Edited and used by permission.

Mercy Ciniraj and her husband, Paul, live in India. Together they serve in a ministry committed to bringing the gospel of Jesus Christ to India and the Third World.

38

Wanting What He Wants

Linda Highman

"You've never had a date? Why not?"

I was an eighteen-year-old college freshman when that infuriating question was first asked of me.

"No one ever asked me out," I replied. *The answer's obvious,* I thought. *Dating is a two-way street, after all. And as they say, it takes two to tango.*

The looks of pity on my roommates' faces, however, were only the beginning of their efforts to make me over. They began by plucking my eyebrows and teaching me how to style my hair. It didn't get me a date the next day, but I certainly felt better about myself.

Only God knows, but perhaps their efforts did eventually pay off. A group of my fellow choir members and I began to have lunch together. Usually the group was mostly girls, but it sometimes included one friendly, nonthreatening fellow with a sweet, tenor voice. At first we were "just friends," but then we became "campus brother and sister."

Finally, one Saturday night while standing on a chair cleaning my closet, I turned to my best friend with the confession, "I love him." I'd never said that before. Startled, I stopped for a few seconds of serious consideration. Then I confirmed the fact. "I love him!"

I immediately had questions. And they would continue for the next two-and-a-half years. *How does he feel about me? What kind of relationship do we really have? Is this what God really wants for me? Is this His best for me—His plan for me?*

The tension in these questions distracted me from my studies and drove me to play the dating games that had always disgusted me. However, my daily devotional time—a habit begun when I was eleven—kept me grounded throughout this time.

The Christian university I attended reserved one room on each dormitory floor as a prayer room. These rooms were available 24/7 for anyone who needed a quiet place to pray and meditate. I was there every morning on my knees, asking God for guidance for my life.

One day during my Bible reading, I was struck by Psalm 37:4: "Delight yourself also in the LORD, and He shall give you the desires of your heart" (NKJV). I memorized it in a moment. At first I thought it meant that God would grant me what I wanted. But what did I really want? Did I really want the boy? Was he really "the one"? I found myself praying, "Lord, I *want* to want what *You* want me to want."

Gradually, I realized the true meaning of the verse. As I put God first in my life and made Him the center of my heart, He would put His desires there. God doesn't grant or fulfill our desires just because we read His Word every day. Rather, He gives us those desires to fire our imaginations and motivate us to follow the big plans that He has for each of us.

As I learned to pray for God's desires to be mine and for His perfect will to be accomplished, the events of my romance played out. Eventually, in God's timing, I married the sweet tenor and we began our saga of shared careers, life's disappointments, and God's abundant joys. Through it all, the echoes of Psalm 37:4 have sustained and guided me.

Delight yourself in the Lord, *and He shall give you the desires of your heart. (Psalm 37:4* nkjv)

Linda Highman and her husband were colleagues for forty-two years as they taught in Christian schools in Oregon. Now retired, they continue in education as volunteers and tutors.

39

The Journey

MEREDITH PAZ

I'm a big believer in having dreams and goals in life. But I know a young man who had a dream that I wanted to do everything in my power to stop. The man was Matthew, my firstborn child. As a boy, he got along well with his sisters, was responsible and trustworthy, always appeared on the honor roll, and never really did anything substantially wrong. He even received a $42,000 scholarship to a private university in his senior year of high school. My dreams for him were being fulfilled.

But before going to college, Matthew had another dream—take a gap year and travel internationally by himself. He wanted to do this using as few resources as possible and not always depending on a reliable or specific itinerary. He also wanted to understand how people lived outside our hometown.

My response was, "How will you survive? Why do you want to do this?" I feared for his safety; I feared for his life.

But when your son is nineteen years old and over six feet tall, he really can do anything he wants. After pleading with him not to go, I tried to reason him out of it. I told him all the reasons I didn't want him to go, but he didn't change his mind.

Matthew left for his journey on the first day of that year. Five minutes after saying a teary goodbye, I called a dear friend and told her what had happened.

"You're going to have a story too," she said. "Ask God to give you a promise from the Bible every day and journal what He shows you."

That day, God gave me this promise from Psalm 32:8: "I will instruct you and teach you in the way you should go; I will counsel you with my loving eye on you." This verse became my prayer for Matthew over and over again. I prayed that God would instruct and teach him the way he should go, and that He would counsel and watch over him.

That evening I journaled:

Today, I realized that for the past nineteen years, my life has been nurturing this boy. Protecting, helping, teaching, encouraging, challenging, stretching, paying for and praying for, feeding, guiding, and loving him. And now, Lord, You are his mother and his father. You will be the One to parent him because he is 100 percent out of my hands.

When I woke up the next morning and realized this wasn't a nightmare but a reality, I became fearful again. Then I opened my Bible and found the promise in Isaiah 41:10: "Do not fear, for I am with you; do not anxiously look about you, for I am your God. I will strengthen you and help you; I will uphold you with my righteous right hand."

I remembered something I'd heard a few months before: More than any other command in the Bible, God says, "Do not be afraid." It's what the angels told the shepherds. It's what Gabriel told Mary when he appeared to her and said she was going to bear a child. *Things didn't quite go the way Mary had planned either,* I decided.

Each day God gave me an encouraging word. Even when I was most afraid, God gave me a supernatural peace that couldn't be explained.

Meanwhile, I told my family, friends, and Moms in Prayer group about Matthew's journey. They encouraged me to send out regular e-mails sharing what I knew of his travels along with the scriptures God was leading me to pray so they could pray with me. Soon Matthew had more than fifty families praying for him.

I concluded from Psalm 139 that wherever Matthew was, God was with him. Even when Matthew was far, far away, God's hand guided him and His right hand held him fast.

Day by day and week by week, God answered specific prayers: from preserving Matthew's health while traveling through several foreign countries to providing extra resources that enabled him to continue his journey.

Matthew returned home to our family in late August, after traveling almost nine months and more than seven thousand miles. He accomplished what he'd set out to do, and we came to feel proud of him for the courage and faith he showed on this great adventure. To say it was good to have him home is an understatement.

Even though most people, including me, told him not to, Matthew followed his dream. Three weeks later he began classes at a university, and a few years later graduated.

I went on a journey as well. I went from being full of fear to being full of faith. God spoke to me in promises. He led me by His Word. When I asked Him to direct, protect, and provide for Matthew, He did.

Every day of the journey, I had a choice. Instead of dwelling on my feelings of fear, I learned to think about what I believed to be true. When God makes a promise, I can count on Him to follow through.

I will instruct you and teach you in the way you should go; I will counsel you with my loving eye on you. (Psalm 32:8)

Merideth Paz enjoys hiking new trails, photography, and boogie boarding on any warm sunny beach.

40

Surprising Packages

BETSY SELLICK

A nswers to prayer don't always arrive in the packaging I expect. I grew up living one of those ridiculously blessed lives—the sort that caused people to doubt my honesty and push for a sign of unacknowledged disaster. Living in Northern California where the sun shines almost daily, I had a loving and stable Christian family, incredible health (I rarely even got a cold), and a wonderfully supportive community of friends. My husband came from a more challenging background and often said I "grew up in a bubble."

After our two children were born, however, a disaster appeared out of nowhere. I started experiencing minor seizures. Doctors were baffled. Tests and scans of all types didn't reveal any problematic issues and almost all the antiseizure drugs were useless. A medical explanation was never found. Discouragement crept into my life as I realized my unusually good health wasn't likely to return anytime soon.

Thankfully, after more than thirteen years of multiple medications and extensive treatment, my seizure disorder dramatically improved and my hope and belief for complete healing were restored. I still experience minor, infrequent, and approximately one-minute-long "absence seizures." Just prior to a seizure, I experience an aura, a neurological warning that allows me approximately twenty seconds to prepare myself before the seizure comes on.

Despite the safety factor working strongly in my favor, I chose to restrict my driving and carefully monitor my activities. I certainly wasn't tempted to take up scuba diving, but I occasionally drove short distances from my house for work and errands.

"Aren't you afraid of having a seizure when you drive?" a friend once asked me.

"No," I replied. "When I get into the car, I simply ask God to protect other drivers and me. Just as Jesus cried out on the cross, I also pray, 'Father, into your hands I commit my spirit.'"

One day I had to drive for a work errand. On the way home, I had an aura as I was exiting the freeway. I immediately saw there was no place to pull over on the exit ramp before the twenty-second warning time would be up. As I approached a three-way stoplight on a busy main street, the seizure began. I couldn't control my limbs, and I lost control of the vehicle. I hit the car in front of me, smashing the rear bumper up to the backseat. Next, I crossed four lanes of traffic and jumped the raised median. I hit another car on the opposite side of the street and spun it onto the sidewalk. Finally, my car went over an embankment and hit a tree straight on. When I regained consciousness less than a minute later, I didn't understand why three distraught people were running up the hill toward me. Because they were running the opposite direction from a restaurant that had been closed for years, my first thought was, *Oh, that's crazy! They should have called ahead to find out if the restaurant was still open.* I hadn't yet noticed the tree directly in front of me.

A sweet woman came to my car-door window and frantically asked if I was okay. Just as I was telling her I was fine, I noticed the tree a few feet from my face, indicating my situation was less than ideal. I wasn't pleased to see the hood of my car was wrapped around the tree trunk. The good Samaritan told me about the accident and helped me call my husband. Within minutes, police and firefighters arrived and assessed the damage.

My only physical injury was a slightly bruised chin caused by impact with the steering wheel. However, two other drivers and one passenger were involved. We were all rushed by ambulance to hospital emergency rooms. After an extremely thorough and embarrassing medical exam, my lack of injury was irrefutable. Throughout that intensive emergency-room time, I prayed for the health and comfort of the other three people involved.

The next day a policeman who had been at the scene called me to check on my condition. Both he and the primary doctor who had examined me believed I should have been seriously injured, if not killed. They simply couldn't make sense of just a slightly bruised chin. The policeman also reported on the amazing healthy status of all of us involved. Everyone had been examined and released from the hospital.

"God miraculously protected us," I told the policeman, wanting him to hear that God, because of His love that surpasses understanding, performed this miracle that preserved our lives. "Luck" or "an alignment of the stars" wouldn't take credit for this.

I had, of course, assumed that God would protect me *from* a seizure-related car accident. Instead, God protected me *during* a seizure-related car accident.

Today life isn't "the bubble" it was in the past—and that's difficult. I lost my driver's license and have no current hope of it being returned. Would I choose this frustrating lifestyle? Definitely not. However, I'm willing to accept that my brilliantly wise God has a carefully crafted purpose for me. Though I'm not overly excited about it, my new status of restricted freedom is one in which I trust His plan will best be fulfilled.

His intervention that day provides exciting proof of His closeness, compassion, and power. I confidently believe that God stepped in to work miraculously on my behalf. I'm determined to share my story of God's protection with anyone who will listen: bank tellers, grocery clerks, Costco employees, mail carriers. And now I pray my story of His miraculous rescue will encourage you to depend on God's answer to your call, even if His response doesn't seem to fit your desired outcome or packaging.

"My thoughts are not your thoughts, neither are your ways my ways," declares the Lord. *(Isaiah 55:8)*

Betsy works in the office of their family business while her husband conducts home inspections. Together with a team of volunteers, they raise money for Young Life camp scholarships by organizing Wild Canyon Games, an annual outdoor adventure race in central Oregon.

41

Take It to the Bank

Joyce Frey

One day I felt the Lord nudge me to stop by the bank to inquire about interest rates on a certificate of deposit (CD). We had a rental house we'd been trying to sell for months, but the property had a huge drawback: it was on the corner of a very busy street. We spent thousands of dollars fixing it up on the inside and outside, and we were still spending hours each week maintaining the yard and watering the newly planted shrubs and flowers. So for three months we prayed earnestly for God to send a buyer. Now it was just days away from the real estate listing to expire, and no one had shown any interest in it.

At the bank, the teller directed me to the manager, who turned out to be a friendly young man. When he asked me why I wanted information regarding a CD, I explained the situation about our house and told him that as soon as it sold, we were considering directing some of the money into a CD savings plan.

"Where is the house located?" the manager asked.

I told him.

"My wife and I love that area," he said. "I would like to see your house."

The next day he came to the house and was very impressed.

The busy street didn't seem to bother him at all.

"I would like to bring my wife to see the house," he said. "If she likes it, we'll buy it!"

We were overjoyed, and yet we tried to be cautiously optimistic in case his wife was not as thrilled about it as he was. We prayed for God's perfect will to be done and waited expectantly for His answer—and the young couple's answer.

The next day we got the call. "She likes the house. We want to buy it."

The listing expired the very week the bank manager bought it, so we didn't have to pay a realtor fee. We ended up not investing in a CD, but I realized that going inside the bank that day had nothing to do with that. Instead, it was truly a nudge from the Lord and an answer to prayer for the sale of our property.

My husband likes to say that I sold the house, but we both know it was God. And I give Him all the glory.

To Him who is able to do exceedingly abundantly above all that we ask or think, according to the power that works in us, to Him be glory in the church by Christ Jesus to all generations. (Ephesians 3:20-21 NKJV)

Joyce Frey is a proud grandmother of five grandchildren. In her spare time, she enjoys gardening, traveling, and being with her family.

42

A Prayer, Lord, That I May Pray

Tami Laursen

My daughter, Rachel, was in elementary school when one of her classmates' mothers started relentlessly inviting me to a weekly prayer meeting called Moms in Prayer to pray for our children and their school's faculty. Now, I loved praying. And I knew this would be a way to build my relationship with my heavenly Father while also building relationships with people as we learned to trust God together. I wanted to pray with these women—for our children and their teachers. Yet each time Barbara invited me, I found myself declining, making lame excuses as to why I couldn't go, such as "I want to keep my Fridays free." I came to discover, though, that my real fear was the intimidating thought that if I went to Moms in Prayer, I would have to pray out loud with other people listening.

I declined the invitation for eighteen months, but Barbara was persistent. I finally caved in and told her I would show up at the next meeting. As I drove there, I wrestled with my insecurities about speaking and praying to God out loud. But when I walked into the room, I was met by some of the most welcoming and encouraging women I've ever met. Barbara turned out to be the coordinator for that Moms in Prayer group. As we started praying together, I clearly saw that these women were real prayer warriors. Over time, through receiving God's grace and sharing part of my prayer life with these women, I was able to face my fears of praying out loud.

When Rachel was in eighth grade, my husband's job required us to move from Puyallup, Washington, to Clackamas, Oregon. I missed my Moms in Prayer group in Puyallup tremendously, so I asked God to help me find another group of prayer partners. One day, nearly a year later, I was leaving Rachel's high school when I heard someone call my name. I turned around and a woman introduced herself and said, "I want to invite you to our Moms in Prayer group."

My jaw dropped. I was so excited that I rushed home to tell Rachel the news. Yet, just as I had before, I found myself creating excuses for why I couldn't make it to the meetings. My reasons were the same as they had been before, and the main one was my insecurity about praying out loud in a room full of women I didn't know. For three months I didn't go.

However during this time, God removed my pride and excuses. I realized this fear about praying out loud shouldn't hold me back. He put a longing in my heart to be in authentic relationship with fellow women so we could pray for our children. I had to go to Moms in Prayer in faith that God would provide those kinds of friendships while teaching me how to be comfortable praying in front of people.

It felt like déjà vu when I walked through the front door of the meeting room of the Clackamas Moms in Prayer group and was greeted by a loving and enthusiastic woman named Suzanne, with whom I instantly connected. All the other women were genuine and loving too. I could hardly wait to go back the next week. As I got in my car to leave that first meeting, my heart felt full of gratitude to God for taking me there.

During our meetings, we were encouraged to pray with someone different each week. I was always amazed with how God seemed to place me with just the right woman to pray with and get to know better. All twenty of us have come to know each other well through praying God's Word for our children and seeing God faithfully intercede in our lives.

All too soon, Rachel headed to college, as did many of the other children of the moms in our group. Yet we continued to meet. Each week, as Rachel shared prayer requests with me, this group of women fell in behind me with their prayers and support. Their passion for prayer helped me give the Lord the burdens I brought through the door each week. Week after week we saw Him provide scholarships to colleges and acceptances to medical schools. He helped heal family relationships and so much more.

Though most of our children are now adults, we still meet on a weekly basis during the school year to pray for them. Suzanne and I have been prayer warriors and dear friends ever since that very first meeting. We've laughed and cried together, and we've prayed our children through their high school and college years.

I stand in awe of God and His willingness to help me have a personal relationship with Him and others through the power of prayer. God, the only perfect Parent, provides His children's best when I, as an imperfect earthly parent, depend on Him. He has assured me of who I really am to and in Him. He's a trustworthy God. I can leave my fear and insecurity in His loving and capable hands—even about how to pray.

Two are better than one, because they have a good return for their labor: If either of them falls down, one can help the other up. (Ecclesiastes 4:9-10)

Tami Laursen loves to build friendships centered around praying together. When God answers, she always has people to celebrate with.

43

Powerless Statues

GUADALUPE GOMEZ

The suffering began when I was twenty-five years old. The doctors told me the severe abdominal pain was gastritis, but as years dragged on, they found it was an ever-growing cyst in my bladder. The pain became so excruciating that for days and sometimes weeks I was completely unable to get out of bed. Doctors wanted to operate on me to try to find all that was wrong with my body, but I was scared surgery would make things worse. So I lived with the pain, extreme as it was. Many times it was so horrible I wanted to kill myself.

I have seven children. All are grown, but two were born with intellectual disabilities and are unable to care for themselves. One night, after twenty years of pain, I was determined to take all the pills I had. But once again, as I had every time before, I thought of these two children and decided to hold on to life.

The next morning, a woman named Amanda came to my house. She was from Good Samaritan Ministries. She'd been hosting a Bible study every Wednesday morning for the women in my neighborhood, as well as counseling my daughter and me. She arrived early at my house and asked how I was doing. It was just the two of us, so I broke down crying and told her of my frustration with the physical pain.

"My never-ending pain makes life horrific," I said. "Because of the pain, I hate my life. Trying to deal with this in my way, I've made mistakes that have hurt my family. And because of that, I feel unloved." I also told her of my anger toward God, and how I'd been rebelling against Him in sin.

Amanda prayed for me. She prayed for hope in my life. And as she talked to God, the pain in my body eased. The next day, however, it came back.

I have many statues of saints in my bedroom. A few nights later, I sat there in pain, considering again whether I should take my life. But, instead, I decided to once more beg the statues of the sacred saints to take away the physical agony. I prayed to Our Lady of Guadalupe, to Saint Judas Tadeo, and to my picture of the Lord of Mercy. I thought they represented God. But when they did nothing to alleviate the pain, I decided to stop praying and to quit believing in God altogether.

The next week, Amanda came again to my house for the Bible study. She asked, "How are you, Guadalupe?"

"Not much better," I replied. "In fact, I've completely abandoned faith in God."

"Why?" she asked.

"I prayed to my statues to heal me, but they did not hear my prayers. God did not hear me."

"None of those statues are God," said Amanda. "You can pray *directly to God*." Then Amanda showed me Deuteronomy 32:39 in the Bible, where it says there is only one God. Amanda said we are to pray to Him alone. He is not in a statue. She had me place my hand over my stomach where it hurt, and she placed her hand on top of mine. Then she prayed to the one and only true God, in the name of Jesus Christ, that He would heal my illness and take away the pain. In that moment, the pain started going away. I felt the power of God flow into me. I started feeling dizzy, and then I felt complete peace.

On her next visit, Amanda asked, "How are you doing, Guadalupe? How is the pain?" I gladly told her that the pain was completely gone, not only in that area, but throughout my whole body. I later went back to the doctor who had wanted to operate on me. He did an ultrasound and found there wasn't a cyst in my bladder anymore.

After this healing, I know the one true God. I know there is no other. I tell people that there really is only one true God and to pray to Him alone for help and answers.

Meanwhile, I have made many life-changing decisions to draw closer to Christ. God has given me more patience with my children. I've stopped being rude to them and neglecting them. I no longer curse all the time. I continue to attend the Bible study, where Amanda has shown me love and is devoted to helping me know the Lord. Though I still struggle with sin, as we all do, my faith in Jesus Christ is growing. I'm seeking Him and awaiting more miracles.

I give thanks for what He's done in my life. Jesus healed me.

See now that I alone am He; there is no God but Me. (Deuteronomy 32:39 HCSB*)*

Guadalupe Gomez, Guanajuato, Mexico, "Along the Way," 2014 Spring Edition, *Good Samaritan Ministries*, GoodSamaratianMinistries.org. Edited and used with permission.

Guadalupe Gomez continues to live cyst-free in Guanajuato, Mexico.

44

Time for a New Terry

JUDY NEIBLING

"Don't you do what Ginny did," my brother Terry angrily warned me.

It was the mid-1970s. We were at our parents' home in Maryland talking about giving our hearts to Jesus, which our older sister, Ginny, had recently done.

I was nineteen years old, and I was thinking about giving my heart to Jesus too. But I was far from telling Terry that. He was the big brother I fought with growing up but dearly loved. I understood where he was coming from. All three of us siblings grew up going to church every Sunday, but none of us had been close to God. A year after Ginny shared her newfound peace and joy with Terry and me, I began to talk about God with him. But he thought the whole thing was a "bad idea."

Soon afterward, Terry's infant daughter died, and his marriage crumbled. He left Maryland for Wyoming and started a new life there. Meanwhile, Ginny and her husband, Dan, joyfully decided to pack their bags and become missionaries in Papua New Guinea with Wycliffe Bible Translators. Then God called me to become a staff member for Campus Crusade for Christ (now called Cru). I served in the US Virgin Islands, Mexico, and then, after meeting my husband, Ed, in the Philippines.

The four of us started praying for our Terry.

I'd heard of fasting as a young believer, so I decided to fast and pray during one meal a week for Terry's salvation. I usually fasted during lunch on Friday unless I was pregnant or nursing one of our three children. Sometimes my prayers were impassioned, but more often than not they felt feeble. Nonetheless, the habit of fasting reminded me to pray.

Whenever Ed and I visited the United States, it was difficult to figure out what to talk about with Terry. We had very little in common. He was either working in the oil fields of Wyoming or driving across the country in trailer rigs. Every few years, I would write to him about giving his heart to Jesus. He never seemed interested.

This went on for years, but one day I wrote in my journal that Terry had told me, "I'm not a heathen" and that "knowing Jesus sounds good." The same journal entry included my study of the book of Romans, where the apostle Paul wrote, "My heart's desire and my prayer to God for [the Israelites] is for their salvation" (10:1 NASB). I also wrote, "Is my brother's salvation my dearest dream? Yes—and my prayer."

Four years later, I heard Joy Dawson of Youth With A Mission (YWAM) speak at a conference in Manila, Philippines. She recommended that we pray not only for the salvation of our loved ones but also that they would become Christians of influence. I added that to my prayers for Terry.

Ten years after that, while driving a truck through Florida, Terry looked for a radio station to tune in to, but he could only find a Christian one. As he listened, the speaker said something that led Terry to conclude that Christianity might be true.

Not long afterward, Ginny, Dan, Ed, and I were on furlough from our mission work, and we decided to meet in Kansas, where Ed is from. Ginny was celebrating her fiftieth birthday while we were there, so Terry flew in as a surprise. He brought magazines to show us what he'd ordered from that Christian radio station. Then one night during our visit, he had a dream that I was standing on the other side of an open door, calling to him to come through.

The next evening after dinner, each of us shared again with Terry how we came to know Jesus. Dan asked Terry what he thought salvation would be like, and my brother answered, "It's like going through a door." We all agreed. Terry didn't tell us he'd answered that way because of the dream he'd had the night before. We thought he might pray with us and put his faith in Christ at the table that night, but he didn't. Ed asked him if he knew what to do if he wanted to begin following Christ, and he said he did.

On the phone with Terry a few days later, I heard the news I'd longed to hear for twenty-one years. Alone in his cabin out on the plains, Terry had prayed, "My Father in heaven, please forgive my sins. Thank You for Your Son dying on the cross. Please come into my heart and be my Lord and Savior."

"Immediately, spiritual things started happening," Terry now recalls. He's never said what those things were—we only know that a spiritual transaction took place. Our joyful, peaceful brother became proof of 2 Corinthians 5:17: "If anyone is in Christ, he is a new creation; old things have passed away, and look, new things have come" (HCSB).

Whenever we talked with Terry before he came to know Christ, we were at a loss for words. Now he always has a Bible verse or doctrine in mind to discuss as soon as we start talking. Our animated conversations can go on for hours. He studies Scripture with others and earnestly ministers in a local prison with other church members. He loves to pray and tell coworkers, friends, and strangers how they can know Jesus. Terry has become a Christian of influence!

Twenty-one years of prayer and seventeen years of fasting one meal a week—how it all seems like nothing now that Terry knows Jesus. Having this "new" brother is one of the greatest answers to prayer in my life.

If anyone is in Christ, there is a new creation; old things have passed away, and look, new things have come. (2 Corinthians 5:17 HCSB)

Judy Neibling and her husband, Ed, are missionaries with Cru and served for several years in the Philippines.

45

Do Not Worry

DEB MEYERS

It was the week before Christmas when we got the call. My husband, Ed, was diagnosed with cancer. Even though we knew his form of cancer was slow growing and treatable, I was gripped with fear and anxiety. My first instinct was to reach out to family and friends to ask for prayer. But my husband wanted to wait until after the holidays to tell anyone—to give him time to digest the news, research treatment options, and meet with specialists. It would end up taking several months for all that to happen.

Satan does some of his best work when we feel isolated. I felt paralyzed by fear, and I wondered, *What if he dies? What would my life be like without him?*

But God was speaking to me too.

I received a little devotional book for Christmas, which I began to read. After the New Year, several of my church's small-group Bible studies picked up again. It was uncanny that in the devotional book and each of the Bible studies, the focal Scripture passages were all centered around God's commands to not worry, to not fear, and to trust Him.

These messages started coming on a weekly basis. It seemed as if everywhere I went, God was telling me, "Do not worry; do not fear; trust Me." Then they started coming even more frequently as the weeks turned into months, and Ed and I grew closer to having to make decisions about his treatment. I shared these God-incidences with my husband each time they happened, and we took courage in them. But sooner or later, I always found fear creeping back into my mind.

One day I received a phone call from one of my closest sisters in faith.

"I know this is going to sound strange," she said, "but you keep popping into my mind. I keep hearing the words, 'Don't be worried or afraid.' I feel weird about calling you, but is there something going on that I don't know of and about which you should stop worrying?"

I didn't know whether to laugh or cry. "Yes, something is going on, but I can't tell you about it yet. God has been sending me this message quite often lately, and He's apparently using you today to deliver it. I will tell you more as soon as I can, but in the meantime, please keep Ed and me in your prayers. God knows what it's all about." I hung up the phone and called my husband to tell him this latest message. As we both chuckled, I realized that the time had come. I needed to start taking God at His Word. It was time to put my faith into action and fully trust that God was walking with us and would provide the strength we needed to face this trial, regardless of the outcome.

My husband and I had been praying for four specific things: that God would guide us to the right specialist, help us choose the best treatment, minimize the treatment's side effects, and grant total healing. After learning my husband was a good candidate for all available treatment options, we decided to talk to a world-class surgeon and radiation oncologist. My husband was leery of surgery because of its risk factors, and because the surgeon spoke of his patients as if they were statistics. In contrast, my husband felt instant rapport with the radiation oncologist. The best form of radiation treatment quickly became obvious, and our initial prayers for guidance were answered.

After two months we finally had a plan in place. We were at last prepared to talk with friends and family and ask for their prayers. It was hard facing the reality that I had very little control over anything in this situation, but that led me to turn to God for comfort and strength and to gratefully accept the love and support of our community. As we continued to lean into God's Word—which kept telling us, "do not worry, do not fear, and trust Me"—we found ourselves living more fully in the present moment.

Going through cancer with my husband gave us several gifts: We learned to cherish each day and to tell others how much we loved them and why they were so important to us. We also learned to slow down and savor the beauty of a sunset and the first buds of spring. We found ourselves seeing with fresh eyes what was truly important in life, while what was superficial and unimportant became readily apparent.

We took a walk one day, holding hands and laughing at our dog's antics. Suddenly I realized how many moments of joy we were experiencing in the midst of these difficult circumstances.

Although the cancer was still there, God was transforming the way I thought about and responded to it. I was learning to trust in the reality and presence of God in my daily life—in His ability to guide, strengthen, and speak to me through His Word, prayer, and friends of faith.

When the day of treatment finally arrived, a sense of calm came over me. A friend came and sat with me during the procedure and we prayed that God would guide Ed's medical team. We prayed that the treatment would kill all cancer cells and that Ed would experience minimal side effects. We gave thanks for the availability of world-class healthcare and for health insurance. We gave thanks for the knowledge that God was with us and walked before us.

The procedure was supposed to take two hours. It took four.

During that wait, I repeated the words, *Do not worry, do not be afraid, I am with you always.* And in those moments, trusting by faith in God's promises, I felt His Spirit calm my heart and grant me peace.

I never sensed that the "do not worry" message was about God promising miraculous healing. It was a message about trusting in God's faithfulness to be present with us—regardless of the outcome.

Nearly two years have passed since that day; I thank God that Ed's treatment has proven to be successful. He still experiences some side effects of treatment, which is to be expected. Although I don't think about the cancer on a regular basis, we continue to pray for Ed's ongoing healing.

I give thanks for the lessons in trust that God taught me through this process. Now I know that when new trials assail me, I can trust in God's presence and strength to see me through them. Because facing life's fears and worries is a daily battle, surrendering to God is a daily choice. Only when I am surrendered do I experience complete peace in His presence. And it's because of the gift of His presence that I can more easily do as Paul said: "Rejoice always, pray continually, give thanks in all circumstances; for this is God's will for you in Christ Jesus" (1 Thessalonians 5:16-18).

The LORD himself goes before you and will be with you; he will never leave you nor forsake you. Do not be afraid; do not be discouraged. (Deuteronomy 31:8)

Deb Meyers enjoys facilitating discipleship small groups and helping others grow in faith. She and her husband enjoy wilderness adventures.

46

Hope for Tomorrow

RON MARLETTE

Drugs and alcohol. I was twelve years old when these became my ways to escape the pain of life, family addictions, and homelessness. At the age of fourteen, I started dealing drugs. I dropped out of school because it got in the way of my lifestyle. Over the next seven years, I fell deeper and deeper into an abyss of addiction and crime.

When I was twenty-one, the police came to visit me. While they were looking for my stash of drugs, I was looking for a place to hide. They didn't find what they were looking for, but they left me a note that read, "We'll be back." That note terrified me because I was dealing a large quantity of drugs. In that one moment, as I held that note in my shaking hands, I realized I needed to change my life.

With no hope in myself for recovery, I checked into a drug and alcohol recovery program and decided to try for something that had eluded me for ten years: a clean and sober life. It didn't take long to realize this also meant staying away from the people, places, and things that were associated with my drug life. If I didn't, there would always be temptation drawing me toward my old ways.

Soon after being released from rehab, I ran into a friend who used to regularly invite me to church. I always thought she was crazy, considering she knew what kind of lifestyle I was living. This time she invited me to attend a Billy Graham crusade. I decided to go. It was there in that stadium, sitting among thousands of people, that I first heard a clear presentation of who Jesus was, how He saw me, and how He could help me live a life of peace, purpose, freedom, and hope.

Then and there I asked Jesus to help me live the life that I could not on my own—a life of faith, hope, and love. I started learning about living with compassion, mercy, and grace. I now knew that by grace I was saved, through faith—and this was not from myself, but was a gift of God (Ephesians 2:8). I started a recovery support group at the church I was attending, passionately believing that since I found victory over my addictions, I could help others as well.

Sensing an overwhelming burden to do more, I went back to high school and received my diploma. Then I went to Multnomah University for a four-year degree, becoming the first person in my family to graduate from college. God continued to bless me. I married my wife, Jennifer, and we now have five grown children. Soon after my college graduation, I was asked to launch a satellite mission in Solano County, California, to serve the homeless and addicted. Fifteen years later, Mission Solano's Bridge to Life Center stands as a testimony of God's faithfulness to His vision of showing grace, mercy, and compassion.

Many times over the years, those who came to Mission Solano have told me, "Ron, you don't know what it's like. You don't know how hard it is to change and get off drugs and live a clean and sober life."

I smile and say, "Oh, I think I know what it's like. Let me tell you what it will take. And, if you're ready, you too can live a new life."

I then share with them how God's love met me where I was. How He gave me the hope and help I needed to stay sober and clean up my life. Most importantly, I let them know that He gave me the hope of a life in Him and a passion to help others. I share God's Word to me: "If anyone is in Christ, he is a new creation; old things have passed away; behold, all things have become new" (2 Corinthians 5:17 NKJV).

I know the hope of Jesus Christ at Mission Solano, and I love sharing it. It starts with a hot meal, a clean bed, and a new start. Yes, I know what it's like and, better yet, I know in whom to find the strength, freedom, and hope for tomorrow.

It is by grace you have been saved, through faith—and this is not from yourselves, it is the gift of God. (Ephesians 2:8)

Ron Marlette is the founding CEO of Mission Solano Rescue Mission. He and his wife, Jennifer, have been married for more than thirty years and have five grown children. Mission Solano has been called "the Rescue Mission of the Future" because of its public and private partnerships and holistic programs.

47

No Slings Attached

DAWN JESKE

My daughter, Hannah, was a cheerleader her sophomore year in high school. One day during a stunt, Hannah caught the full weight of the flyer above her. *Pop!* she heard as the girl landed in her arms. It was her left arm. We thought it would be fine in a few days, but three weeks later, it had become excruciatingly painful to even move. We took her to her regular doctor, who couldn't figure out what the problem was. She recommended we see a pediatric doctor, and later, an adult orthopedic surgeon. No one could figure out the source of the pain. We went to a physiatrist, who provided no answers, and then visited our city's professional basketball team's sports doctor. He did an experimental procedure on Hannah where he drew blood and then reinjected it into her area of pain. This didn't work either.

Hannah did several rounds of physical therapy, including a technique where metal instruments were rubbed against the painful area. All these therapies were tremendously painful but solved nothing. In addition to having two CT scans, she had three MRIs, where needles injected dye into her body (Hannah *hates* needles), plus a bone scan, which required doctors to inject her body with radioactive dye so they could visualize all of her bones. We even saw a tumor specialist, just in case.

None of them found an answer for her pain. By now, Hannah was sick of seeing doctors and didn't want to look for an answer anymore because the therapies hurt so much. So she bore the pain and wore a sling on and off for more than three years. During this time she couldn't play sports in school or games with her youth group. People started saying she was making the pain up because no doctor could find anything wrong. After three years, Hannah started wondering if they were right—if she was only imagining the pain.

Hannah saw one last doctor, who proposed she had a rare condition called chronic regional pain syndrome. Over time, her limb would get hot, swollen, and red. Then it would soften and deform. "Sometimes, people even get an amputation," he said.

Hannah asked for exploratory surgery, but the doctors wouldn't do it because they couldn't find any medical evidence that something was wrong.

Sometime later at a Bible study Hannah and I attended, I felt God tell me to ask the group to pray for Hannah. They did, fervently asking God to heal her and to help us find an answer. The next day, I searched online for a professional in chronic pain syndrome. As I scrolled though dozens of names, I felt led to click on a certain physical therapist's website. It said he had fifty years of experience. I read, "If you want to stop your pain at the source rather than just strengthening the surrounding muscle, we are the experts." I called and explained Hannah's story to the receptionist. "When can I bring her in?" I asked.

"That physical therapist is semi-retired," she said. "And right now he's on an extended vacation in the San Juan Islands. Would you like to see his associate?"

"No," I said, sensing inside that I needed to pursue the physical therapist himself. "I want to see the man with fifty years of experience."

"I'll call him and let him know," she said.

An hour later I got a call from the San Juan Islands.

"Hello," said the therapist. "I'm really interested in your daughter's case. Tell me more."

I told him everything.

"I think I know what's wrong with her," he said. Because Hannah would leave for college in two weeks, he scheduled an appointment for the following week. He left his vacation early to meet with us.

Meanwhile, Hannah was exhausted from seeing doctors and had basically given up hope. Plus she didn't want to miss a shift of work to make another doctor's appointment.

"I'm not going," she said to me. But I knew the Lord had steered me to find this therapist's website. When I told her I would replace her wages, she agreed to go.

The night before the appointment, I attended a friend's birthday party and asked the group to pray for the upcoming session. There in the restaurant, they stopped the celebration and took turns individually praying for Hannah for several minutes.

The next morning Hannah, her father, and I found ourselves sitting in yet another waiting room. By this time we had a one-inch stack of medical papers from the past three-years of long appointments, endless research, painful treatments, and failed attempts to fix the pain. As we looked around we noticed a Bible on the coffee table. I wondered if the therapist was a believer. If he was, it made sense that I'd felt so drawn to call him.

The physical therapist listened to Hannah for an hour, and then began pointing out details about her arm that we'd never noticed before. It was as if he saw the interior workings of her arm in his mind. After observing for a few minutes, he said to Hannah, "A tendon popped off your bone and tore. Scar tissue is rubbing against the bone, sliding back and forth like pulling a knot on a string of yarn through a needle. The way you hold yourself to protect your arm from pain is actually perpetuating the problem."

The therapist knew exactly what was mechanically wrong with her and, moreover, understood her pain.

"It hurts so bad that you want to cut your arm off," he commented.

We reminded him she was leaving for college in two weeks.

He said, "We'll have this taken care of before then."

We didn't believe him because of all we'd been through, but he took such a personal interest in her that we decided to trust him. Hannah began the new treatments he prescribed. He had his associate rearrange his schedule so he could assist us. Every day over the next two weeks, the pain level decreased. Hannah was able to control the pain, even making it completely go away if she did the exercises and movements she was supposed to do.

She was able to do the small things again, like pick up her backpack. She no longer had to wear a sling just to walk around.

At the end of the two weeks, I went to the physical therapist to thank him.

"God has given me this gift," he said. "I'm so happy to be able to use that gift to help people." He was so humble and such a servant of the Lord. God truly answered the prayers of the women in Bible study and all the people at the birthday party in orchestrating this appointment and putting us together with the one person who could help her.

Hannah had to endure a lot of nasty things in hopes of finding healing. She's also a hard worker, so sometimes she felt as if she wasn't doing her part. She wasn't able to sleep well at night, so she felt exhausted all the time. And there were many times when she was simply emotionally overwhelmed. It was draining to have such pain as a daily reality for so long.

But now everything is changed! If her arm and shoulder ever hurt, she knows exactly what exercises to do to remedy the pain. Hannah has now completed her second year of college and can do all the activities she used to do—and activities she's wanted to do for years, such as being a theater assistant, carrying costumes, lifting heavy objects, moving props, and dancing hip-hop and swing. She hasn't had to wear the sling again.

Because her healing was delayed, we as a family pondered the story of Lazarus. Jesus purposefully waited four extra days before going to Bethany where his friend lived. So we too choose to trust that God had a purpose in Hannah's injury and the timing of its healing. In an instant, Mary and Martha went from being desperate, hopeless, and exhausted to being filled with gratitude and wonder by God's mighty working.

We too rejoice and wonder in God's ability to take a seemingly hopeless situation and, in His wisdom and mercy, bring us hope and allow Hannah back into a renewed, active, and normal life.

Pray in the Spirit on all occasions with all kinds of prayers and requests. (Ephesians 6:18)

Dawn Jeske is a devoted mom, wife, and dog owner. She works as a medical professional and serves as a volunteer in women's ministries.

48

Twelve Minutes

Faye P.

One rainy Saturday afternoon I was on a quick shopping trip to the mall with my friend, Tami, to buy a gift card. I stuck my smartphone into a pocket in my jacket as we walked to the outside information kiosk to find the location of the store we needed.

As we stood at the kiosk talking to a clerk, a young man came very close to me for a few seconds. I joked about it and then shrugged it off. It wasn't until after Tami and I were walking out of the store with the gift card that I reached into my jacket pocket and realized my phone was gone.

I knew a smartphone was replaceable, but the precious pictures of my granddaughter and even her bite marks on the case of the phone weren't. The color drained from my face. I started to panic, but Tami reassured me that I must have just dropped the phone in her car. But when we retraced our steps all the way back to her car and looked inside, we found no phone.

We went back into the mall and asked a manager to call security, all the while fervently praying that an honest person would find it and turn it in. Then we retraced our steps back to the store—still no phone.

Throughout this time, Tami was calling my phone. On the third call, someone answered.

"Hello?" It was a security officer in the mall.

Tami and I looked at each other with shock and relief. My eyes got huge with tears, and then I did a jig right there in the mall while praising God. We didn't care who saw or heard us. God, my heavenly Papa, needed thanks right then and there!

Then we sprinted to the mall's security office to retrieve my grandbaby-bitten smartphone. After talking with security in the office, we deduced it was the young man at the kiosk who had pickpocketed me. The security officer used the term "apple picking."

Upon realizing my phone was security locked, the thief had thrown it down a set of stairs where a thoughtful little girl and her mom found it and turned it in at a nearby store. They gave it to the manager, who then brought it to the security office.

All of this happened in a matter of twelve minutes. We needed to catch our breath, so we sat down. Neither one of us was really surprised that God provided, but we were in awe as to how faithful He was in answering our prayers so quickly. Even though my request seemed trivial in the grand scheme of life, Papa cared enough to handle something that mattered to me, even though it was just a phone.

With our God, no prayer is too big, and no prayer is too small!

Praise be to the LORD, for he has heard my cry for mercy. The LORD is my strength and my shield; my heart trusts in him, and he helps me. My heart leaps for joy, and with my song I praise Him. (Psalm 28:6-7)

Faye P. is a business owner and full-time grandmother. Her passion is people and her joy is to do her best to add value to them. The blessing of her life is her precious granddaughter.

49

His Eye Is on Me

JUDY PUGEL

Twenty-two years into my marriage, my husband was admitted to the hospital with a malfunctioning liver. Unless God intervened, he was expected to die.

Alone in my bedroom I cried out to God for my husband's healing. In that moment God's presence surrounded me, and I sensed He was telling me that He was with me in my husband's illness. I thanked Him for coming, gave myself to Him, and told Him I would do whatever He wanted me to do—just as I had done in my first month of marriage.

You see, my husband wasn't the man I thought I knew. In our twenty-two years of marriage, he'd demonstrated a will of iron. He used fear to control our daughter and me. This had resulted in our complete isolation from the body of Christ by the time of his hospitalization. My daughter and I hadn't been allowed to attend any church for more than four years because, according to him, no church was doctrinally sound enough to even be called a church. He was convinced that he was protecting us from going down a slippery slope of doctrinal error where we would surely make ship-wrecks of our souls.

I'd cried out to God for His help—and He came. For twenty-two years He gave me the strength to serve, love, respect, and submit to my husband.

My husband came home from the hospital and was placed on hospice care. I had an overwhelming desire to pray for three things: (1) I prayed God would restore his mind a little every day, (2) I prayed He would completely heal my husband's body, and (3) I prayed God would deliver him from his underlying fears, which had not only done great damage to our marriage and family but had controlled him his entire life. Fear truly had the strongest death grip on him.

God began to answer my first two requests. After a few days, I noticed little changes in his mental processes. Then his blood pressure went up. After two weeks, he came off of hospice care and had a stent placed in his liver. After two months, his memory and strength returned.

I prayed and hoped God would answer my third request—healing for his underlying fears and troubled past. Despite two godly men counseling him, he remained silent and unwilling to communicate. Instead of humbling himself and being willing to take an honest look at his life, he insisted that he was fine and in no need to understand what had happened to him. Rather than moving forward, he pulled us back into the way life was before his illness—a life filled with fear, isolation, and control.

But everything had changed for me. God had made it clear to me that He wanted to deliver us from the fear we were living under. I took a stand to go forward with God rather than step backward into fear. My daughter and I began attending a church nearby, and I continued to pray and wait for God to do something in my husband's life.

One day I came home to find my husband changing the lock on our front door. He was taking control of what he perceived to be my rebellious stance. I knew I wouldn't be allowed back into the house until I agreed to submit to him and obey his orders.

He didn't realize that because he was locking me out, God had opened wide His door to me. My daughter and I moved in with my sister. It was now God's turn to take control but His control was full of love, provision, comfort, and hundreds of small and big ways of showing me His eye was on me.

The following Sunday, we attended my sister's church. During the service, we went forward for prayer. I told the young woman who came to pray with us that I'd been locked out of my home. I didn't say anything more. I was amazed as the woman began to pray about specific things that had happened in our home over the past few months.

"Mom, how did she know?" asked my daughter on the way home.

I could only answer, "The Spirit of God was praying through her."

Now at this time, I'd been a Christian for forty-two years. I was a seminary graduate. I'd studied the doctrine of God. I knew and believed that God was everywhere and He knew everything. But as I experienced God's love in that moment, He became more than a doctrine to believe in. He became real and personal. I knew beyond a shadow of a doubt that God had been with me in my house all these years, listening, watching, knowing, and caring.

The next Sunday I attended my sister's church again. But this time I asked God for a word from Him. I'd never asked Him for such a thing, and I didn't know what I was asking for when I prayed for it. Nonetheless, He answered my request.

Before the beginning of the sermon, the pastor stood and said, "God has a word for someone here to today. You've been isolated from the body of Christ. You've been going through the most difficult time in your life. God wants you to know the body of Christ is here for you."

I immediately began weeping at those words. God was giving me His promise of provision through His people.

Three months later and without a word, my husband filed for divorce. A year into the divorce proceedings, during a two-week period of time, I prayed every day, "God, show me how much You love me."

One Sunday I sat back down after the church service was over, and a young man with Down syndrome walked up to me. He asked me in the sweetest voice if he could pray for me. I nodded.

"God, show this lady how much you love her. Amen." Then he said: "I saw you sitting here all alone. I know what it's like to be alone."

Again, God heard my prayers! He used this young man to show me that His eye was on me, and that He is creative and personal in how He shows His love.

At the time of this writing, five years have passed since my divorce. They have been difficult years. I have yet to find sustainable work because being a homemaker, homeschooler, and violin teacher during our marriage wasn't enough to create a career path.

God has promised He has work for me to do. I've waited on Him, knowing He is always working *good* things together for lovers of Him.

While I can't say I sailed through this trial with robust faith and unfailing trust in God, I can—I *must*—say that He is faithful and His Word is true.

Doubts have assailed me at every turn. At times I've been overcome with fear and anxiety. But I've learned to live by worshipping, praying, fasting, reading my Bible, and continually asking God for help.

I've been living every day with God, knowing what matters most is that He loves me and His eye is on me.

Nothing in all creation is hidden from God's sight. (Hebrews 4:13)

Editor's note: A year after this story was written, God blessed Judy with John, a faith-filled, loving man who was recently widowed. Their wedding was a celebration of God's faithfulness to both of them.

Judy Pugel speaks to women of all ages. www.daughteroffaith .webs.com

50

A Dime in God's Pocket

Beki Duke

We can't out-give God. You can't be too generous with Him. I've tried. I met Jeff, my husband of thirty-four years, at summer camp when we were in our early twenties. We married eight months later. We had three kids in four years. We bought a dairy farm, adopted two more kids, and kept living life at a fast pace. I often found myself praying the words from Matthew 6:10: "Father, may Your will be done in our lives as it is in heaven."

Just when it felt like life was settling down and we could ride the waves for a while, God prompted Grandma Duke, Jeff's mom and a hardworking grandma of twenty-four grandkids, to consider purchasing the old, vacant Trout Lake K-12 school to turn into a summer camp. And she wanted us to be in on it. Always a dreamer, she began by wondering, "How does one go about turning an old school into a summer camp?" "God and grit" was her answer.

The next few months were filled with serious and strange conversations between Jeff and me. Our roles had temporarily reversed. While I felt ready to jump headlong into this life-changing purchase, certain that God wanted us to sell our dairy farm and partner with Grandma Duke in this endeavor, Jeff did everything to fight against it. He loved our dairy farm. He loved the cows and country lifestyle. So he resolutely stood on the notion that we were never selling it.

Yet through a series of miracles, and because of his love for God, he changed his mind. When a stranger approached him about buying a piece of our land that we thought would never sell, Jeff knew his dairy farming days were over. He was offered $140,000 for the land—exactly the price of the old school. Again, we were praying, "Father, Your will be done."

Never in my wildest dreams did I think we would waltz into a room of school-board members with a meager $2500 in earnest money, an offer so simple it looked as though a fifth-grader could have written it, and five land sale contingencies. But that's exactly what we did. And just days later, we made the phone call to the board, saying: "We now have the cash to buy the building!"

We sold our coveted family dairy farm of sixty acres, including the 4-H animals our kids dearly loved. Like a bunch of hillbillies, we proudly moved into the old and doomy-looking school building with all our junk and a forty-horsepower John Deere tractor.

The old home-economics room became our main room because it had a sink, countertops, some cupboards, and a place for a stove and refrigerator. By adding a carpet remnant, couches, a table and chairs, and a few more furnishings, we did well turning it into a livable home. Our kids' friends either thought we were crazy or cool. What other family had a gym, tennis court, and multiple showers and bathrooms, and put their beds in classrooms?

This fixer-upper of a school became more than a home. It developed into a simple yet significant Christian camp and retreat center. We named it Camp Jonah, where "Kids laugh, hearts change, and God smiles."

The name Jonah came from the way we teased Jeff during our initial weeks debating whether to go forward with the purchase. We'd say, "So, Jonah, are you on board yet or are you going to jump ship again?" Jeff thought Tarshish looked so much better than Nineveh. We related to the truth in this book of the Bible: When Jonah followed God, his small obedience made a huge difference in the kingdom of God. And from time to time living in the school seemed not so different than being in the ugly and stinky belly of a fish.

The years of watching Camp Jonah grow into our dream— God's dream—have been beautiful and hard. Yet every time we have a need, God provides. When our commercial dishwasher broke down, a donor stepped forward to replace it. When we asked God for a four-by-four crew-cab pickup, some friends drove in and handed us the keys to theirs. When our bookkeeper saw an upcoming deficit of $18,000 in the forecast, a check came in the mail for that very amount. This was our story from the start. God's will was being done.

After fifteen years of living in the home-economics classroom, Jeff and I moved into a travel trailer. I realized we were getting older (having grandkids will do that to a person), so I took comfort in the fact that Jeff and I owned the camp property. I thought that if the road got too tough, or if we couldn't pay the bills, or if we just wanted to retire, we could sell everything.

But one day God spoke to my "Jonah" husband as he was praying in his favorite prayer spot—our Jacuzzi. Jeff felt a heavy sense that God was with him in the water, telling him that we were to donate the property to Jonah Ministries.

We had discussed this in the past, but had always quickly put the idea aside. *Of course God wouldn't have us donate the property,* we thought. A few days later, Jeff told me that he'd made a deal with God. If I brought a "certain topic" up with him within a week, we were meant to do something about it. My soul knew exactly what this certain topic was. I hesitated, knowing that if I said it, my earthly security would be gone.

"Is it about donating the building and land to Jonah Ministries?" I asked with great hesitation.

After a few moments of both of us sitting in shock and silence,

Jeff latched on to this like a pit bull. Within days we handed the title over to our governing board. I felt sick at heart. We were now totally broke. We had no earthly treasure. The board worked out salaries for us, and I worked hard to put a smile on my face. I realized I had to accept this new adventure.

Thanks to Jeff's persistence and encouragement, my smile became real. I slowly realized that what God really wanted was simple obedience. I was going to enjoy the peace that comes from simply saying yes to Him. All we were doing was giving back to God the title to property that had been His all along.

Camp Jonah now hosts more than 2500 people per year; more than 300 of which are campers. More than 2300 are retreat guests. We host hundreds of local people at no cost for community events, including the Trout Lake Fair, church activities, youth-group retreats, and supervised visits for foster children.

Throughout the years there were times my heart ached for a home of our own. We often prayed that we could somehow purchase the house next door, especially since having neighbors so close was very stressful at times because we were running a camp. Every time I felt the ache, I would quickly give over our living situation to the Lord. As I've sought God's will in my life, a certain tried-and-true measure of trust has grown in His ability to provide.

Not long ago the neighboring property suddenly went up for sale. Through generous donors, an amazing grant, and God's grace, Jonah Ministries purchased it. Jeff and I now live in that beautiful, often-prayed-for miracle home! We often ask each other when we'll have to "check out of our presidential suite." The view from every north-facing window is of the majestic Mount Adams and the glorious Trout Creek. The noise from Camp Jonah's guests make us smile. Our house is often full of staff, guests, and grandchildren, who fill every nook and cranny of our hearts. Once again, our faithful Father stepped in and answered our prayers His way.

We got caught up in His wild dream, and we've been living in the middle of a miracle ever since. We've come to realize that doing the hardest thing is sometimes the easiest choice when our prayer remains, "God, may Your will be done." We're certain that simple surrender pleases Jesus, and that the blessings we're enjoying today are just a dime in God's pocket.

> *Blessed are those who trust in the LORD and have made the LORD their hope and confidence. They are like trees planted along a riverbank, with roots that reach deep into the water. Such trees are not bothered by the heat or worried by long months of drought. Their leaves stay green, and they never stop producing fruit. (Jeremiah 17:7-10 NLT)*

Beki Duke is the cofounder and camp coordinator of Jonah Ministries' Camp Jonah, a Christian camp and retreat in Washington state, where "Kids laugh, hearts change, and God smiles." www.campjonah.com.

51

Love Always

For nine months I was a single mother of my son, Zayne, before I met and fell in love with Dave. Dave and I married a year later, and he adopted Zayne as his own. At the time, Dave was working hard toward a college degree, so Zayne and I spent every day together, just the two of us. We'd go to parks, the zoo, and the museum of science every chance we got, talking, laughing, and playing together the whole time.

When Zayne was five years old, Dave and I started having children, but those years with just the three of us helped us form a special bond that could never be broken.

As Zayne grew, our conversations changed and became about more complex things such as relationships. He seemed to have no problem telling me anything or asking for my advice. After he moved out, he still called me regularly to share an idea, talk about an event, or just to say, "I love you, Mom."

One day, he started talking about a woman he'd met at work. Paige was a single parent of a young son. She'd revealed to Zayne her fear that she would never find a man who would love her and her son. Zayne told her not to give up, as he too was the son of a single mom, and his mom had met and married a wonderful man who became his father.

Soon Zayne's relationship with Paige blossomed. He brought her over for dinner one night to meet us. She was a beautiful woman with a kind demeanor, and we got along well. When it appeared there might be a wedding in the near future, they told us that they were doing things in a less-than-ideal order, and that a baby was on the way. They decided to become husband and wife before the birth of their child. Her parents and Dave and I were the witnesses at their ceremony. They would hold a big summer wedding after the baby arrived.

They had a beautiful baby girl and named her Emma. After she was born, I began feeling an animosity from Paige, but I didn't know why. She'd tell me I wasn't holding Emma correctly. I made a comment that I'd raised three children, and that I'd held many babies in my lifetime and had never been told this before. It seemed to make matters worse. When we arrived at the bridal shower before the summer wedding, Paige graciously hugged my mother-in-law and daughter, but turned her back to me. During the party, Emma was passed around so all could admire her. But when she was finally put into my loving hands, Paige came over and took her out of my arms, saying she needed to change her diaper. When she finished changing her, she passed her into someone else's arms. Every time I got close to Emma, Paige snatched her away for some reason.

After that, I was steaming inside every time we were together. She avoided eye contact and would only talk to me briefly if I spoke to her first. I was shocked at her treatment of me. I felt like my son had married an enemy—and she was now part of our family. Zayne's marriage to Paige began affecting my relationship with him. I felt angry, hurt, and sad.

Finally, the day of the summer wedding arrived. I was instructed to not hold the baby during the wedding. I felt terrible. I was supposed to be happy for Zayne, but instead a dark cloud hung over me because of Paige's horrible treatment of me.

In the past I simply distanced myself from people who treated me badly. But how could I even think to cut off my relationship with Paige, the woman whom my dear son Zayne had married and who was the mother of my precious granddaughter?

I began to pray. I told my trusted friend all that had occurred between Paige and me. We prayed about it together. When I opened my Bible, God took me to Mark 10:7-8. Jesus says, "'A man shall leave his father and mother and hold fast to his wife, and the two shall become one flesh.' So they are no longer two but one flesh."

In that moment, I remembered my love for Zayne. Neither he nor the rest of my children had always acted wonderfully. But even when they were rebellious, sassy, and mischievous, and I in turn felt angry and disappointed, I still always had a love for them that went beyond their actions. God showed me through this verse that if I loved Zayne that much, and if he and Paige were one flesh, then I was to love her the same way.

After talking with Zayne and praying for wisdom in this situation, I reached out to Paige. As I took steps of faith to make things right with her, our relationship was restored and transformed by God's love. Since then, I've learned to ask for forgiveness and pursue making things right when we have misunderstandings.

Zayne and Paige have asked me to babysit my grandchildren on a regular basis, and I'm deeply involved in their lives. Recently Paige told me she trusts her children in my care more than she trusts her own parents, and that she deeply appreciates and loves me.

In the thick of the emotions of feeling terrible and at a loss for what to do, I truly believed nothing would help. But I was wrong. God showed me that I could *love always*, and that with Him all things are possible.

Love is patient, love is kind. It does not envy, it does not boast, it is not proud. It does not dishonor others, it is not self-seeking, it is not easily angered, it keeps no record of wrongs. Love does not delight in evil but rejoices with the truth. It always protects, always trusts, always hopes, always perseveres. (1 Corinthians 13:4-7)

Jacqueline B. is a new Christian and lives to serve God. Looking back on her life, she realizes that God has guided and protected her for His purpose. Her new purpose in life is to love people for Jesus.

52

Miracle Awakening

Larry Poland

Remote is hardly a sufficient word to describe the tall forest jungles of Peru in South America. The jungle is so dense that only two months before I entered it, I heard a report that a Boeing 727 had crashed into its trees. It took a search party six weeks to find the wreckage—even though the authorities knew the mile radius of where it went down. The trees had literally swallowed it.

When I went to Peru, I took a commercial flight over the Andes jungle to the city of Pucallpa, then a small-plane flight into the heart of the jungle, and then a half-day cruise on a riverboat to get the fifty or so missionaries and me to Lake Tipishca. We were seventy-five miles from the nearest *unpaved* road.

The occasion that brought me this far off the unpaved beaten path was an annual four-day retreat and planning session of missionaries from a Florida-based missions organization. I was to be the main speaker. The missionaries had traveled there from a number of South American countries.

I spoke on the first day in the morning and sensed the spiritual climate was cold. Even the proximity to the Equator couldn't warm it. At first the attendees were kind to each other, but an afternoon business session revealed that a number of them had some pretty awful attitudes. One man suggested they shut down their mission efforts in more than one country. I watched as discouragement and despair filled the room.

Moreover, I witnessed strife within the families. I was graciously given a bedroom in one of three homes that had been built for the permanent missionary families assigned to the mission base and Bible school at Tipishca. Built crudely of native material, the home's thin walls couldn't prevent me from hearing the unkind way the husband spoke to his wife and daughters. It was terrible, and I nearly wept.

I called the heads of the mission together the following evening. I said that I thought we were wasting our time with the teaching sessions each morning. I shared my perspective that the spiritual climate was cold, the missionaries were just going through the motions, and my messages were falling on deaf ears. I recommended that we suspend the well-planned schedule and, instead, meet for a time of confession, prayer, and healing until God's presence was felt and heeded.

The leaders were surprised at the suggestion. They'd put a lot of effort into planning the conference. Nonetheless, they agreed to the plan. As leaders, we spent time in prayer, asking God to do a special work in all our lives. At the next conference meeting, the head of the mission announced the suspension of the schedule.

The next morning, all fifty of us met in the largest room of the Bible school. I gave a short devotional from Ephesians 5, titled "The Holy Spirit and Interpersonal Relationships." I slowly read through the passage and highlighted how relationships controlled by the Spirit of Christ are marked by harmonious communication, praise and thanks to God, and mutual submission to each other. The message wasn't spectacular, and the passage was surely not new to these veteran servants of Christ.

Then I announced we would be spending an indefinite period of time in prayer together. I suggested we begin with silent self-examination. We bowed our heads. After a few minutes of silence,

I heard sniffling. It was a bit strange. Soon it sounded like an upper respiratory virus has suddenly broken out in the room. I looked up and people were weeping. I let the praying and weeping continue for a while.

"Now I think it would be good to focus our prayers on confession," I said quietly. "If anyone has anything to confess, please feel free to share it with us all."

After a few moments of pause, the wife of one of the three couples stationed at Tipishca stood and burst out, "O, God, forgive me! I've hated Eileen [I don't remember the name she actually used]. I have envied her talent..." And then she broke down and wept aloud.

The room went silent, but the sniffling continued. Then the father of the home where I was staying stood and cried, "O, God, forgive me! I've been a wretch to my wife and daughters." He sobbed his way through his prayer.

What happened the rest of our time that morning defies description. One after another, these dear missionaries stood and confessed their bad attitudes, rebellion toward leadership, lack of faith in tough circumstances, and more. Not one of them had a dry eye. I was dabbing the tears running down my cheeks as well.

With this long session of confession now clearing their hearts, I felt a tug to launch a time of singing praises to God. It was incredible. With no instruments, one person after another launched a hymn, gospel song, or chorus a cappella, and the room almost burst with the passionate harmony. It was a Tipishca version of angel choirs. It was *heavenly.*

The morning passed quickly. We were stunned when one of the leaders announced it was lunchtime.

I suggested to the group, "Before you leave the room, give someone a hug and make anything right that needs to be resolved."

I'll never forget what I saw next. The woman who had confessed her jealousy found "Eileen," and they wept on each other's shoulders. A burly missionary approached an executive from the headquarters office in Florida, lifted him off the floor in a bear hug, and confessed, "I've hated everything that came out of that office. That is wrong. Please forgive me." They wept with each other.

Filing to the next building for lunch was an exercise in spiritual buoyancy. The laughter and interaction was light and joyful. But there was one dimension I didn't expect and had never witnessed before.

In the New Testament book of Acts, the author describes a scene where the Holy Spirit fell on those gathered on the day of Pentecost: "All those who had believed were together and had all things in common; and they began selling their property and possessions and were sharing them with all, as anyone might have need" (2:44-45 NASB). This historical and miraculous event was a stunner. God supernaturally worked in their hearts and they *willingly* separated from ownership of their most prized possessions.

That started happening in the lunch line. A missionary noticed his friend shooting pictures and commented that his camera looked new. The man shooting the photos described the features of his brand-new camera, and then lifted it off his neck to give to his friend.

"No, no!" the friend protested. "I have a good camera." Arguing that this new camera was better than his, the man made another attempt to get him to keep it.

I saw one woman admire a necklace with fabulous beadwork that another woman was wearing.

"Where did you get that beautiful necklace?" she asked.

"The women in the village in my Bible study made it for me and gave it to me as a present," she replied. "Here, I'd like you to have it." Ignoring protests, she lifted the necklace over her head and placed it around her friend's neck.

That afternoon, an entirely new and revolutionary spirit marked the scheduled business session. The same men and women who were riddled with anger, defeat, and discouragement twenty-four hours earlier were now discussing and developing a master plan to expand their efforts to take the good news of Jesus Christ to the entire continent of South America.

You may be asking, "Was this really a miracle?" *Definitely.* It was a concert of miracles. I've studied human behavior from every angle, even at the graduate level, from psychology, sociology, economics, history, and political science to theology. I've never read about or heard a therapy proposed that is capable of changing *an entire community* of fifty people this radically in just three hours. I know not one behavioral dynamic that can bring a group of human beings to open confession, repentance, restitution, mutual sharing and bonding, and self-sacrificing beneficence in 180 minutes—only God could have done this.

There is one thing I am certain of. There is power in the Spirit of God working through His Son, Jesus, in the hearts of those who are occupied by Him through faith. The Spirit of God makes life a miracle walk for those who trust the Savior and allow Him to control and empower them. If you don't already believe, I challenge you to do so now and surrender to Him.

All those who had believed were together and had all things in common; and they began selling their property and possessions and were sharing them with all, as anyone might have need. (Acts 2:44 NASB)

Excerpted from Larry W. Poland, PhD, *Miracle Walk* (Tucson: Entrust Source Publishers, 2012), pp. 79-83. Edited and used by permission.

Larry Poland is the founder and chairman of Mastermedia International and founder of the National Media Prayer Breakfast. For three decades, his organization has provided counsel on the faith community to leaders in film and television. www.mastermediaintl.org.

Epilogue

The Prayer that Changed Everything

Suzanne Frey

When I was a child, my parents brought me to church, and I am very thankful for that. Consequently, I've always believed God exists. As I shared in my story "Feast or Famine" (chapter 11), it wasn't until my college freshman year that someone explained to me that God wasn't a passive Creator—a smiling "grandfather in the sky" or an entity that was only worshipped by going to church. God is alive; He is Someone who loves me and created me to know Him personally.

I began to understand that my selfish choices (what the Bible calls "sin") separated me from a relationship with God. Even though I was basically a good person, being good could never be enough to sustain a personal relationship with Him. But, being the gracious God He is, He provided a solution to bridge the gap—Jesus Christ.

Through Jesus, I've come to know and experience God's love in a vibrant and personal way. God sent His Son, Jesus Christ, to die on the cross to pay the penalty for my sins that I may have true freedom in Him.

That evening during my freshman year, when this was made clearer to me, I knew I wanted to begin a relationship with Jesus.

I knew this was missing from my life, and so I invited Jesus to live fully in my heart and be my Savior and my Lord.

I prayed a prayer similar to the one that follows. If you're unsure where you are with God or if you've never had a personal relationship with His Son Jesus, I encourage you to pray this prayer:

> Lord Jesus, I want to know You personally. Thank You that You love me so much that You died on the cross for my sins. I invite You into my life and ask You to be my Lord and my Savior. Thank You for forgiving my sins—every single one of the mistakes I've made—and giving me eternal life. Change me, heal me, and give me a fresh new start with You.

If you prayed that prayer, tell someone you know who loves Jesus or write to me. I want to help you grow in your personal relationship with Him. Please remember:

> The power you read about in this book
> is not in prayer itself,
> but in the God to whom you pray.

Prayer Was Never Meant to Be Complicated

Prayer is just talking with God. Just like I love having coffee with friends and we take turns talking, God loves it when we talk to Him and listen to Him. He also often speaks to us through His Word, the Bible.

I recommend you write down your prayers in a notebook, journal, or on your computer. Be sure to date your entries and, when God responds, write that down too.

Search for and ask God to lead you to scriptures you can pray through (like in the book of Psalms). Praying God's Word is praying God's will. Here's an example of personalizing and praying

God's Word using Ephesians 3:17-19. You can pray this way for yourself or loved ones.

> I pray that you, being rooted and established in love, may have power, together with all the Lord's holy people, to grasp how wide and long and high and deep is the love of Christ, and to know this love that surpasses knowledge—that you may be filled to the measure of all the fullness of God.

God, may I [Suzanne] have the power to understand, as all God's people should, how wide, how long, how high, and how deep Your love is. May I experience the love of Christ, though it is too great to understand fully. Then I will be made complete with all the fullness of life and power that comes from You, my God.

Most importantly, when God answers your prayers, thank and praise Him! Write down how and when He answered. When appropriate, share your joy with others.

My prayer and hope is that you will see God's marvelous doings in your life and have the courage to share your story as well.

If you would like to read more comments about these stories and how they've inspired people, please visit our website. And if you have an amazing story of answered prayer and would like to submit it for future projects, you'll find guidelines on the website.

www.SuzFrey.com

If you've been encouraged by the stories in this book, the contributors and I would love to hear from you. Please e-mail your comments to:

Suzanne@SuzFrey.com